A
GOURMET'S
GUIDE TO

CHEESE

A GOURMET'S GUIDE TO

CHEESE

CAROL TIMPERLEY
&
CECILIA NORMAN

Photography by
GRAHAM TANN

HPBooks
a division of
PRICE STERN SLOAN
Los Angeles

ANOTHER BEST SELLING VOLUME FROM HPBOOKS

HPBooks
A division of Price Stern Sloan, Inc.
360 North La Cienega Boulevard
Los Angeles, California 90048
9 8 7 6 5 4 3 2 1

This book was created by Merehurst Limited
Ferry House, 51/57 Lacy Road, London SW151PR

Commissioned and Directed by Merehurst Limited.
Recipes by: Cecilia Norman, Carole Handslip, Dolly Meers and
Kerenza Harries
Photographer: Graham Tann
Food Stylist: Sue Russell
Home Economists: Dolly Meers and Annabel Hartog
Color reproduction by Kentscan, England
Printed in Belgium by Proost International Book Production,
Turnhout

Timperley, Carol.
    A gourmet's guide to cheese / by Carol Timperley & Ceci-
lia Norman.
        p.   cm.
    ISBN 0-89586-848-2
    1. Cheese.   2. Cookery (Cheese)   I. Norman,
Cecilia.   II. Title.
    TX382.T56   1990
    641.3'73—dc20   89-19794
                                                        CIP

Contents

INTRODUCTION 7

CHOOSING CHEESE 8

STORING CHEESE 10

COOKING WITH CHEESE 11

PRESENTING A CHEESE BOARD 12

DRINKS TO SERVE WITH CHEESE 14

FRESH CHEESES 16

BLOOMY RIND SOFT CHEESES 22

ENRICHED CHEESES 26

WASHED RIND CHEESES 30

BLUE CHEESES 40

UNCOOKED PRESSED CHEESES 50

HARD, COOKED CHEESES 60

GOAT'S MILK CHEESES 66

SHEEP'S MILK CHEESES 72

SOFT CHEESES WITH NATURAL RINDS 78

PROCESSED CHEESES 82

DIPS 84

STARTERS 86

MAIN COURSES 94

SALADS 106

DESSERTS 110

BAKING 116

INDEX 120

Introduction

The art of the cheesemaker is one of delicate balance. To produce a perfect cheese, with the right depth of flavor, the most mouthwatering texture and delicious aroma, depends on many factors. The milk—from cow, sheep or goat—the breed of animal and the type of pasture all have a bearing on the end result. So too do the complexities of making and maturing the cheese.

To enjoy good cheese is to enjoy variety, contrast and subtlety. There's a cheese for every palate and for every occasion, from the mildest, blandest types, through a whole range of rich, mellow and buttery flavors, to the most pungent, sharp and salty cheeses at the far end of the flavor spectrum. Then there's an astonishing choice of colors and textures to enhance eye and palate. From firm handsome Cheddars through to crumbly, pale Wensleydales; from the soft white curds of Ricotta, to the soft, melting nature of ripe Brie or Camembert. Veined cheeses, charcoal-coated cheeses, cheeses wrapped in leaves—the delights to be discovered are endless.

Cheese originated as an economical way of using up surplus milk, and different countries have developed their cheesemaking and eating habits in different ways. The French serve it after the main course, before dessert; a habit which is becoming increasingly popular elsewhere. Italian pasta wouldn't be the same without a scattering of Parmesan; while the mild crumbly English cheeses melt obligingly to make a wonderfully smooth Welsh rarebit.

With so many types to choose from, cheese can be enjoyed in an infinite variety of ways. Savor it to the full by itself, with bread or crackers, or as a partner for fruit. Complement it with a glass of wine; or let it add its own special note to a hundred-and-one different dishes. However you use it, cheese belongs in a class of its own.

Choosing Cheese

Cheese, like wine, is one of life's great pleasures. Pierre Androuet, the French cheese expert, even goes so far as to say, "If I had a son who was ready to marry, I would tell him 'Beware of girls who don't like wine, truffles, cheese or music'."

Sadly, it is one which is all too often unheeded and many an otherwise enjoyable meal is marred by badly chosen, ill-kept and ill-matched cheese and wine. Yet with just a little thought and care, a cheese board can be the highlight of a meal, capable of compensating for any culinary lapse.

The trick is not to be overly ambitious. Tiny slivers of a dozen or more cheeses are neither appetizing nor complementary: too many flavors and textures all competing for attention merely become confusing and result in a lot of dried-out, unusable leftovers. For an average-size dinner party of six people, four cheeses are more than adequate and the possibility of serving just one superb cheese alone should never be discounted.

Quality should always be the first consideration when selecting cheese. It is worth seeking out a good cheese shop whose stock is kept in carefully controlled conditions. A shop like this will be able to advise you on your choice and should have a wide range of clearly labelled cheeses in stock, including more unusual varieties. Always ask to taste first before you make your decision—a reputable cheese shop will be delighted to oblige. Be flexible in your selection: if the Brie you'd set your heart on isn't in top condition, substitute a Camembert or a Coulommiers.

The first rule of shopping for cheese is never to buy anything in less than prime condition. Ask for your portion to be freshly cut and look first at the cut surface of the whole cheese. It should have a fresh appearance, and no telltale sweatiness, cracking or hardness, all of which indicate that the cheese is drying out.

It's a good idea to feel soft cheeses if you can. They should be springy to the touch and when ripe should be evenly soft from center to edge.

Check that soft cheeses are not too runny. Smell is another good indicator of quality, so sniff your sample of cheese before you taste. It should have a fresh smell, redolent of its particular variety. Reject any that have a hint of ammonia, as they are past their best.

Selecting for a cheese board

Here you should address yourself to the question of balance. A cheese board should be balanced with the other courses of the meal, which means taking into account the type of food being served (Is it strong and spicy, light and fresh or somewhere in between?); the wine which will accompany it; and the relationship between the cheeses themselves. The single, most important factor is never to serve cheeses which require a lighter wine than that which has been drunk with the main course as this has an unpleasant effect.

This, of course, assumes that you will serve the cheese before the dessert, French-style. The reason for this is that few cheeses consort happily with sweet dessert wines; most need something drier or fruitier to offset them to advantage.

Texture, as well as flavor, needs careful thought. The ideal cheese board includes at least one hard or semihard cheese, perhaps a traditional English cheese like Cheddar or Cheshire; one semisoft cheese, which could be one of the milder, washed-rind cheeses; one very soft cheese, perhaps a chèvre or a bloomy-rind specimen; and the fourth possibly a milder blue or a cheese with a *cendré* (ash) coating.

Cheese should always be eaten in ascending order of strength to be fully appreciated. And it's worth noting that soft, semisoft and blue cheeses are tasted by pressing them against the palate with the tongue, while hard or sharp cheeses are tasted on the tip of the tongue. In this way variations in consistency and flavor are apparent. If you think your guests may be uncertain about which cheese to try first, then unobtrusive numbered labels are a helpful idea.

Cantal (hard)

Murol (semisoft)

Bucheron (chèvre)

Roquefort (blue)

An appropriate selection for a cheese board.

Storing Cheese

Overall, it is best not to buy a larger quantity of cheese than you can reasonably eat within a couple of days. This ensures that you will enjoy the cheeses at their best. If you should happen to acquire a whole cheese it may be possible to keep it for more than a year, uncut. It's a tricky business however, as the cheese must be kept in the correct conditions, in a cool, moist ventilated room; and needs regular turning and wiping if it is not to deteriorate.

The length of time a cheese can be kept depends on its moisture content. Fresh cheeses which are high in moisture should be used within a couple of days. Take note of the sell-by date if you buy these cheeses in sealed cartons. Once it is past, the cheese will soon start to spoil. Keep near the top of the refrigerator in the carton, or in a plastic bag.

For most other cheeses, the vegetable drawer of the refrigerator provides the best temperature for storage. Soft bloom-rind cheeses, like Brie or Camembert, should be kept in their boxes or on a plate. Cover the cut sides only with plastic wrap. These cheeses should not be stored for more than a few days. Semisoft to hard cheeses keep longer and the hard grating cheeses like Parmesan, either grated or as a piece, will keep for several weeks. Wrap all these cheeses tightly in foil or plastic to keep out the air. (Use freezer paper rather than plastic wrap.) Different types should be wrapped separately and strong tasting varieties should be kept away from foods. If mold spots develop, cut them off. They will not affect the rest of the cheese.

Cheese which has been bought sealed in plastic may begin to sweat. Remove plastic and blot the cheese dry with paper towels before rewrapping.

Remove cheese from the refrigerator 1 to 2 hours before serving so that it has time to reach room temperature. Cheese bought for same-day consumption can be kept under a cheese dome, although these should not be used for longer storage. Prop the lid up slightly to allow water vapor to escape.

Cooking with Cheese

Cheese is a very versatile ingredient and adds interest and flavor to all manner of dishes including sauces, soufflés, dips, quiches and pizzas. It can be used in baking, and deep-fried it makes a delicious starter in its own right. Of course, cheese is not limited to savory recipes, for it can be successfully used in cheesecakes, mousses and other desserts. The selection of gourmet recipes in this book explores the versatility of cheese to its fullest.

As with wine, it is a mistake to assume that poor quality cheese will undergo a radical metamorphosis once heated. The better the quality of the cheese, the better the finished dish will be.

Careful cooking pays dividends, because cheese separates at 150F (65.5C) and if cooked for too long becomes leathery and tough. When melted by itself it tends to become stringy. The texture is better if the cheese is mixed with a starchy food, such as bread crumbs or potatoes, or added gradually to a sauce. Hard cheese cooks better if it is first grated, although crumbly cheese can be added to a recipe in small chunks. Avoid ready-grated cheeses of the type found in supermarkets, however. These are impregnated with a non-caking agent and although convenient, quickly lose any flavor they once had.

Some cheeses melt better than others. Crumbly varieties such as Lancashire, Stilton or Cheshire are good in soups; while smooth types like Mozzarella and Bel Paese melt down to a pleasingly elastic consistency for pizza toppings. A finely grated hard cheese like Parmesan is perfect for sprinkling on soup or pasta, because the fine particles melt readily and mix so easily into the dish.

Cheddar, an excellent all-around cooking cheese, shreds well and gives a good flavor to sauces and soufflés. Soft cheeses such as Brie or Camembert add interest to quiches, and you can use Leicester or Double Gloucester to add color. Stilton keeps its characteristic flavor when cooked and melts well. Gruyère and Emmenthaler are the classic fondue cheeses.

Mozzarella is the classic pizza topping.

Presenting a Cheese Board

Valençay (a cendré) is served on a separate board.

A carefully balanced, well-displayed cheese board, with a selection of appetizing accompaniments, makes a perfect pause before dessert and is guaranteed to revive the appetite of most diners.

It's worth taking time to arrange the cheese board attractively, although there's no need to overdo the decoration. There are two key facts to remember: the first is that cheeses are attractive in their own right (or should be if you've chosen correctly); and the second is that they are living, breathing organisms which require oxygen.

Despite the fashion for wooden or marble boards, you can present cheeses on almost any material, provided it has a large enough surface area to allow air to circulate between the cheese and prevent them from impregnating each other with their flavors. For this reason the very best way to serve cheese is on a wicker tray, which may be lined with leaves or straw mats to protect it. Because blue and *cendré* cheeses are by their very nature dominant, it is best always to isolate these on a separate surface if possible. Likewise, provide a separate knife for each type of cheese. If the same one is used for all, the cheeses will not retain their individuality.

The overwhelming temptation to treat a cheese board like a still-life arrangement is to be discouraged. A few grapes between the cheeses are acceptable, but not more. Arrange the cheese board an hour or so before the meal and place it, covered with a lid or piece of cloth, in a cool, but not cold, place.

Accompaniments

What to eat with cheese is another thorny subject. Bread or crackers? Buttered or unbuttered?

Washed-rind and blue cheeses are probably best eaten just as they are, with a knife and fork, but many people prefer an accompaniment of some sort with other types.

A good solution is to offer a choice of bread or crackers. Fresh, crisp French or Italian bread is the ideal, preferably quickly heated in the oven to refresh its crust just before serving. Rye and black breads or brown, sturdy whole-grain breads are other possibilities. Creamy cheeses are also good with a light fruit or nut bread.

A selection of plain crackers or semisweet whole-wheat crackers should provide something to suit most tastes. Butter is purely a matter of personal preference, but remember that it does have a tendency to dilute the flavor of the cheese. Always go for unsalted butter; salted is more assertive and interferes with the individual characters of the cheeses.

If a hard English cheese is included in your selection you could also offer celery sticks. A bunch of grapes, or bowl of apples are other refreshing additions to the table.

A simple, attractive arrangement of cheeses on a wicker tray lined with vine leaves, accompanied by grapes, celery and a selection of breads and crackers.

Drinks to Serve with Cheese

Cheeses vary so much in flavor that any attempt to suggest accompanying wines appropriate to each category is practically impossible. There are, however, certain characteristics common to each group which it may be helpful to consider.

Fresh cheeses are almost invariably soft in texture and delicate in flavor. This automatically rules out any wine which is high in tannin as it will overshadow the cheese. Equally, very dry, flinty white wines are unsuitable with fresh cheeses as they create an unpleasant, acidic aftertaste. Something medium dry—white, rosé or an extremely light red—not only offsets the flavor of these cheeses to advantage but allows the palate to appreciate the nuances of their texture. Loire whites such as Muscadet and Sancerre, slightly chilled young Beaujolais or any of the new breed of Blush wines would be acceptable. If the fresh cheese is to be served as a dessert, with fruit, then a dessert wine such as Muscat or Sauternes would be delicious.

Bloomy rind soft cheeses like Camembert and Coulommiers can develop great depth of flavor, which stands up well to most full-bodied wines. Here red is the obvious choice, but by no means the only one. Chaource, for example, could just as successfully be partnered with Champagne or Chablis, while many experts believe that Brie and Camembert go well with good farmhouse cider from Normandy. A more conservative choice, however, would be one of the less refined Burgundies, such as a Côtes de Beaune Villages, or any red made from the Pinot Noir grape.

Enriched or triple crème cheeses generally combine richness with a subtle strength which requires a correspondingly balanced wine. Something assertive, fruity and probably white is called for. Alsatian wines like Gewürztraminer have the strength to counteract the richness of these cheeses, yet being spicy, rather than dry, they do so without detracting from their subtlety. If red wine is preferred, a Bordeaux or Cahors could be the answer.

Washed rind cheeses run the gamut of strengths, and it is more difficult to ascribe family characteristics to this group. A mild, sweet cheese like St. Nectaire cries out for something crisp and white such as Sancerre, Pouilly-Fumé or any of the Upper Loire whites, while a cheese like Maroilles requires a wine such as a really excellent Burgundy. As the vigor of cheese increases, complement it with an increasingly dry wine.

Uncooked, pressed cheeses can, again, vary between delicate mildness and assertive strength. The former are generally best accompanied by good-quality red table wine—nothing too elevated. The slight roughness of the wine adds interest to the cheese and can itself seem smoother and fuller for this foil. Almost any of the generic, jug reds are suitable for this purpose. Here, fruity white wines are probably best rather than bone-dry wines. Steer clear of Bordeaux and look instead to Alsace, the Loire, Australia, New Zealand and California, though avoid anything thin. Stronger cheese in this category can take much more distinguished reds as their relative sweetness has the effect of softening the tannin which can otherwise jar with cheese. Cheddar and Gouda, for example, can take both good Burgundy and some of the softer Bordeaux *crus*. Rich, dark ale produces the same effect at considerably less expense, worth bearing in mind if the cheese is being eaten alone, rather than as a course of a meal.

Hard, cooked cheeses almost all have a background sweetness of flavor which goes well with wine of any description other than bone dry, which inhibits this sweetness. Best of all is something full-bodied, fruity and white like a Beaujolais blanc, a Sauvignon or a good-quality Alsatian Riesling or Gewürztraminer. Soft, warm reds are also good with these cheeses and the regions to look for here are Savoie, Rousette and Chignin. Some of the better quality dark, rich beers should not be discounted for hard cheeses.

Blue cheeses are, without exception, fairly salty and for this reason completely inappropriate with red wine, however mighty. All benefit a great deal more from being teamed with sweet white wines—controversial on the face of it but sensuously superlative. Roquefort with Sauternes and port with Stilton are both, rightly, classic combinations, but any good-quality, sweet or semisweet white wine creates the same effect.

Goat's cheeses are traditionally accompanied by dry white wines, but again this is not an inflexible rule. Coarser, rustic reds can be equally satisfying provided they are not too full-bodied. Sheep's milk cheeses, on the other hand, can take something fruitier and livelier, because of their increased fat content. This also precludes anything which is too high in tannin. Remember, tannin is to fat as oil is to water.

Soft cheeses with a natural rind have a different intensity of flavor, depending on whether they are coated in wood ash or allowed to develop natural molds. The former are in general much stronger and require a full red wine or spicy white wine to be enjoyed to their full advantage. The latter, being more delicate, are at their best with a soft, fruity white or unassertive red.

There are no hard and fast rules about which wine should be served with which cheese, and the suggestions above should be taken as broad indications only. Humbler beverages like dark ale or cider should not be ignored: these can be admirable when matched with cheeses such as Cheddar or Beenleigh Blue.

Personal preference is what counts above all and even experts don't always agree. Some, for example, think that a mature Cheddar served with sherry as an hors d'oeuvre is quite amusing; others deem this sacrilege. Imagination and the courage of conviction are all that really matter.

The classic combination: Stilton with port.

Fresh Cheeses

Fresh cheeses are simply non-aged cheeses which depend solely on lactic fermentation for their character. Cow's, goat's or sheep's milk is rennetted or heated to encourage curd formation, excess whey is drained off and the curds are molded or whipped to smoothness, according to the type of cheese. No further curing takes place. Fresh cheeses are prized for their delicate tanginess and refreshing, moist texture.

COTTAGE CHEESE
A soft cheese, usually made from skimmed, pasteurized milk. After souring with added rennet, the curds are drained and washed. It has less whey extracted than most other cheeses, which accounts for its fairly liquid, granular consistency. Some brands have light cream and salt added to improve the flavor. The end product is a bland, white, slightly acidic, low-fat cheese, much favored by dieters and the cholesterol-conscious. It is available in regular and low-fat.

Cottage cheese can be eaten as it is, with crispbread, crackers, bread or salad, or used as an ingredient in recipes, such as cheesecakes. It is sometimes sieved before use in cooking. It is also available with a variety of added ingredients, such as pineapple, chives, onions and peppers. These flavored cottage cheeses make delicious sandwich filling, with lettuce or watercress for contrasting texture.

CREAM CHEESE
Made in several countries, these cheeses are prepared from light or heavy cream. To qualify as cream cheese they should contain more than 45% milk fat and are consequently quite rich. Cream cheese is recognized by its smooth texture and ivory color. It can be used for spreading or piping, filling and garnishing.

CURD CHEESE
Curd cheese is made from ripened whole milk. It is unsalted and less rich than cream cheese: therefore it is more suitable for cooking purposes. It is sometimes known as lactic or acid curd cheese because of its slightly sour flavor. Consistency varies from fairly liquid to quite crumbly, according to the amount of drainage.

Curd cheese is used in cheesecakes and sweet and savory fillings for flans, crepes, etc. It is also a popular base for dips.

FETA CHEESE
Greece's most popular domestic cheese, Feta dates back thousands of years. The authentic version is traditionally made from unpasteurized sheep's milk, though occasionally from goat's milk or a mixture of the two. Commercial varieties (often imported from Denmark) are almost always made from pasteurized cow's milk, which results in an altogether different—and inferior—cheese.

Real Feta is unfortunately difficult to sample outside Greece as demand there far outstrips supply; also, export restrictions on unpasteurized sheep's milk are stringent. Some small farms however do produce an acceptable version. The white cheese has a crumbly soft texture with small holes and a distinctive sharp, salt flavor. Often it is kept in brine to prevent dehydration. Feta is most frequently used fresh in salads, though sometimes it is used cooked, flavored with herbs, as a filling for Mediterranean pastries.

Sussex Feta

Danish Feta

Greek Feta

Cream Cheese

Curd Cheese

Cottage Cheese with Chives

Cottage Cheese

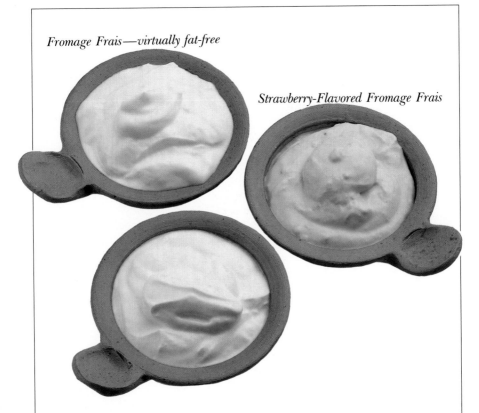

Fromage Frais—virtually fat-free

Strawberry-Flavored Fromage Frais

Fromage Frais—8% fat

FROMAGE BLANC
OR FROMAGE FRAIS

French rennet-curded cheese made from skimmed or whole cow's milk and whipped to achieve a smooth, thick consistency. Fromage blanc cheeses have a fat content varying between 0% and 10%. Because of their versatility they are becoming increasingly popular. They can be used as a substitute for yogurt or cream in cooking and are superb sweetened and served with fruit as a dessert. Fromage frais flavored with fruit, such as strawberry and apricot, is also available.

MASCARPONE

Sometimes spelled *Maschepone*, this unsalted cow's milk cheese from Italy has the consistency of soft butter. Snowy white in color, it is ready to eat within 24 hours and is at its best during the autumn and winter months. Sold loose or in preweighed containers, Mascarpone may be eaten in its natural state or served as a dessert. It is particularly good when flavored with chocolate, coffee, brandy or any liqueur. It has many culinary applications, notably in the preparation of pastries, desserts and vegetable dishes.

MOZZARELLA

A sliceable curd cheese from Italy made nowadays from cow's milk but originally from buffalo's milk. It is made by the *pasta filata* or spun-curd method, which involves heating the curd in water until it becomes elastic and forms strands. These are wound into a ball.

Mozzarella is available throughout the year. This cheese is used mainly for cooking as it has good binding properties. It is perhaps best known as the traditional pizza topping or in the classic Tomato & Mozzarella Salad. It has a mild creamy flavor, pronounced lactic smell and immaculate white color.

PANEER

A traditional Indian cheese widely available in Asian grocery stores. After coagulation the curds are strained and pressed into small, fairly firm blocks. Paneer, or *Panir* is not usually eaten in its natural state but used in the preparation of Indian sweets such as *rasgulla* and *rasmalai,* or grilled or sautéed in vegetable curries.

Danish Mozzarella

Mascarpone

Italian Mozzarella

Petit Suisse

PETIT SUISSE

A rich cream cheese from France—although the name originates from the nationality of a worker in the cheese factory where it was developed, who used to transport the cheese to the Parisian markets. The cheese is made from pasteurized cow's milk enriched with cream to give a fat content of 60 to 70%. Unsalted and bland in flavor, Petit Suisse has a very soft, almost liquid consistency. It is made in portion-sized cylindrical shapes, sold paper-wrapped or in plastic containers. Petit Suisse can be used in the same ways as Fromage Blanc in recipes or served with fresh fruit; it is also available flavored with fruit.

QUARK

Quark is made in Germany, Holland, Great Britain and various other countries, and the spelling changes accordingly. The name simply means curds. It is virtually identical to a Fromage Blanc but with a slightly higher fat content—from 10 to 60%. In Germany it accounts for almost half the total cheese production, and the average German eats about 10 pounds of Quark per year.

RICOTTA

A soft, white, crumbly cheese made from sheep's milk whey left over from the manufacture of Pecorino Romano. It is unsalted and relatively low in fat. Shaped like an upturned basin with a rough pattern on the outside, the curd is compacted so that the cheese can be cut with a knife. It may be eaten plain, dressed with a light vinaigrette, or used as a filling for gnocchi or ravioli. It is sometimes flavored with chocolate.

Ricotta is also available fresh and can be used like cottage cheese.

SAINTE-MARIE

A squat, cone-shaped cow's milk cheese from the Burgundy province of France, Sainte-Marie is thought to have been named after a feast day which falls in its best season: late spring and early summer. Made entirely on small farms from un-pasteurized milk, it can be either salted or unsalted, but should always be creamy and supple rather than firm and crumbly in texture—the latter indicates that too much rennet was added to the milk. Pure white in appearance with a pleasantly sharp nose, Sainte-Marie's refreshing mildness is best appreciated when eaten alone.

Ricotta

Quark

Bloomy Rind Soft Cheese

These cheeses are recognized by their reddish pigmented crusts dusted with white *penicillium* molds and creamy-soft interiors. The degree of surface whiteness depends on the type of milk from which the cheese is made: unpasteurized milk encourages natural, off-white mold while pasteurized milk cheeses are sprayed with artifical pure white spores. Ripening occurs from outer rim to center—usually within one to two months—and opinion differs as to the exact point of ripeness at which they should be enjoyed. As a rough guide, avoid very firm cheeses, and liquid ones, which have been insufficiently drained and can develop sharp notes.

BONCHESTER

Based on a traditional Coulommiers recipe, Bonchester is made in the border country of Scotland from the unpasteurized milk of Jersey cows. The cheese is strictly seasonal as it is made only with milk from grass-fed cattle. When fully ripe, Bonchester has a thick, buttery texture, deep yellow interior and a sweet, balanced flavor. It is made in either 4-ounce or 10- to 12-ounce discs.

BRIE

The history of Brie stretches as far back as the eighth century when, according to legend, the French Emperor Charlemagne first tasted it at the priory of Reuil-en-Brie and thereafter insisted on regular supplies for the palace at Aix-en-Chapelle. While imitation Bries are made in many countries, to bear the name Brie legitimately the cheese must be made in the Seine-et-Marne area south of Paris. All Bries are made in flattish, disc forms of varying depths and ranging in diameter from 13 to 16 inches; their size influences their development. A Brie in peak condition has a deliciously creamy flavor, very rich and fruity.

Genuine farmhouse Bries are imprinted with the marks of the straw mats on which they are ripened. Names to look for include **Brie de Melun** with a salty, concentrated flavor, **Brie de Montereau** which has a mellow, rustic flavor and **Brie de Meaux,** the mildest of the three and regarded by many as the best Brie. Commercially made Bries have less character but can be pleasingly mild. Many variations on the Brie theme also exist, such as Brie with peppers, mushrooms, walnuts, herbs and even blue veins.

CAMEMBERT

Camembert originated in the Normandy province of France and is named after a village in the Orne region where Marie Harel, a farmer's wife, perfected its recipe. Nowadays practically every European country and the United States makes its own Camembert: none however can match the original, which relies on the salty richness of Normandy milk for its unique character. Smaller than a Brie, Camembert has a hearty, fruity flavor of great complexity. It is sold either whole, as a 5-inch disc, halved or, in the case of factory-produced cheeses, in prepacked individual portions.

CARRE DE L'EST

A square, pasteurized cheese from Champagne with a faint, musty aroma and bland flavor. It takes a mere three weeks to mature and it is very consistent in quality. The rind varies from white to orange depending on where the cheese is made.

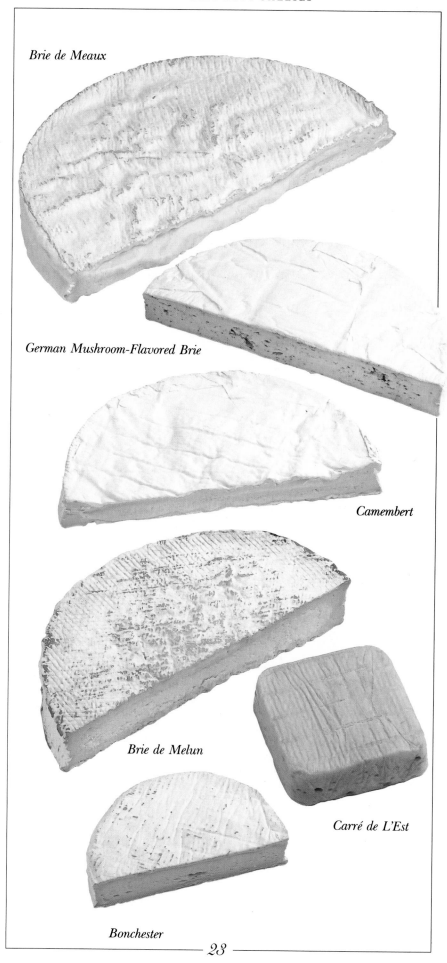

Brie de Meaux

German Mushroom-Flavored Brie

Camembert

Brie de Melun

Carré de L'Est

Bonchester

Chaource

CHAOURCE
A controversial cheese from the Aube *département* of southern Champagne, Chaource's unusual depth, about 3 inches, raises doubts about the uniformity of its development, which can vary considerably between crust and center. Its virtues, however, lie in its refreshing flavor (superb when made from light, spring pasture milk), *chèvre*-like texture and excellent keeping qualities.

COULOMMIERS
Related to both Brie and Camembert, Coulommiers is neither as runny as the former, nor as strong as the latter. Creamy with a distinct fruity tang, the cheese has a nutty background flavor. Made in 5-inch discs, Coulommiers is actually the name of the mold which gives the cheese its shape.

FEUILLE DE DREUX
Made from partially skimmed cow's milk, this rustic hand-ladled cheese from the Île de France is ripened in chestnut leaves. The surface molds tend towards a blue-greyness rather than white and the interior is a dull yellow color. The flavor of this cheese is pronounced and quite fruity.

FOUGERU
A Coulommiers-type cheese ripened in bracken leaves. Larger than its prototype, Fougeru is approximately 9 inches in diameter and weighs around 2 pounds. It is made exclusively on small farms in the Île de France, Champagne, Lorraine and Burgundy, from unpasteurized milk.

NEUFCHATEL
The chameleon of this group in that it changes its shape from manufacturer to manufacturer. Squares, briquettes and cylinders are all common, but romantics should seek out heart-shaped examples. Size and weight vary according to shape but an average cheese would weigh about 3-1/2 ounces. Available all year around, these unpasteurized cheeses are at their best in summer and autumn when their salty smoothness is offset by a delicious savoriness.

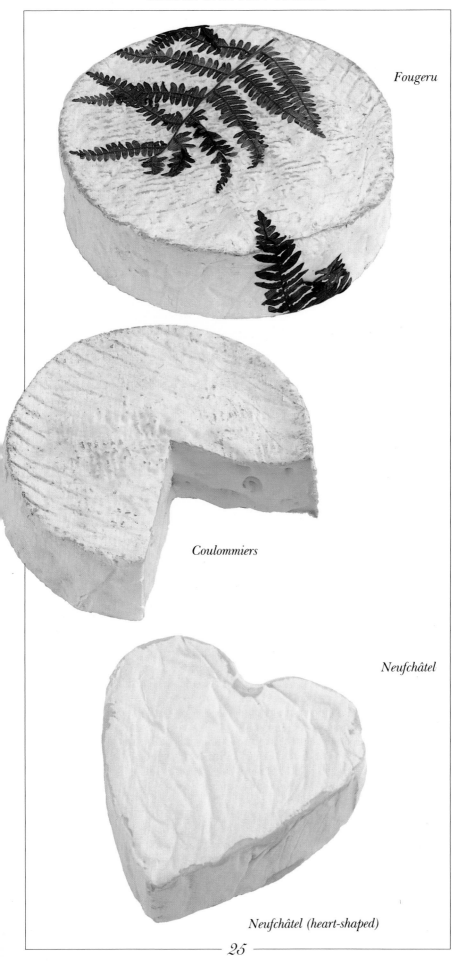

Fougeru

Coulommiers

Neufchâtel

Neufchâtel (heart-shaped)

Enriched Cheeses

Boursault

A branch of the bloomy-rind, soft cheese family which relies on the same manufacturing techniques, these cheeses are made from whole cow's milk, enriched with additional cream to raise their fat content from the standard 40 to 50% to around 75%. Though clearly not for the diet- or health-conscious, their buttery richness is countered by a deliciously rewarding depth of flavor.

BOURSAULT

A small drum-shaped French cheese, about 3 inches in diameter, weighing 7 ounces. Both pasteurized and un-pasteurized versions of this cheese are available. Pasteurized cheeses are packed in a silver and white carton, unpasteurized ones in gold and white. Named after its creator, a cheesemaker based in St. Cyr-sur-Morin earlier this century, the recipe is now owned by the Boursin concern. Boursault has a thin, bloomy rind and is creamy colored. Rich and full-bodied in flavor, this cheese is best eaten when slightly runny.

BOURSIN

A native of Normandy and the Île de France, Boursault's commercial cousin is produced solely in factories from enriched, pasteurized milk. Plain Boursin, can be rather dis-appointingly bland, but garlic-, herb- and pepper-flavored varieties are also made.

BRILLAT-SAVARIN

A relatively modern Norman cheese, invented by Henri Androuet in the inter-war years, it is probably true to say that this is the cheese by which all other triple crèmes are judged. Although soft, it is quite firm in tex-ture with an appetizing aroma and slightly sour, milky flavor. It is made in the form of a thick 5-inch disc.

DELICE DE ST. CYR

A carbon copy of Brillat-Savarin in every respect except that of flavor, which is milder with a nutty back-ground. Delice de St. Cyr is made in small factories in the Île de France and is a good buy throughout the year.

Brillat-Savarin

Boursin with Herbs

Boursin with Peppers

Explorateur

EXCELSIOR

A classic, specialty cheese made by small dairies in and around Norman-dy. It is a soft, double cream cheese with a fat content to match the triple crèmes—72%. It is distinguishable by its irregular, cylindrical shape, firm texture and mild, almondy flavor. It is at its best during the summer and autumn.

EXPLORATEUR

Another Brillat-Savarin-type triple crème cheese which is smaller, firmer and milder than its prototype. It is made in small commercial plants in Brie country.

LUCULLUS

Named after Sulla's consul who was renowed for his lavish style of entertaining, Lucullus is by no means an ancient relic but the product of the last decade. Unlike many cheeses, it reaches its prime during the winter when the cattle's more varied winter stall diet yields milk with a more com-plex, concentrated flavor, capable of withstanding the neutralizing effects of pasteurization. Made in com-mercial plants in the Île de France and Normandy, two sizes are avail-able: the smaller weighs around 8 ounces, the larger, about 16 ounces. The latter is preferable as it develops more consistently.

MAGNUM

A pseudonym for Brillat-Savarin, which is the same cheese aged longer.

PIERRE ROBERT

The creation of the Rouzaire family from Tournan en Brie, a highly re-spected and long-established line of dairymen and affineurs, Pierre Robert is another triple crème cheese to follow in the footsteps of Brillat-Savarin. In common with Lucullus, it is at its best when made in winter when the milk lends the cheese an agreeable, almost salty sharpness. It has very little smell, and it is some-what thicker than other related cheeses, which also accounts for its springy suppleness.

Pierre Robert

Lucullus

Washed Rind Cheeses

These are not dissimilar to bloomy rind cheeses in texture, being mainly soft and semisoft. They have natural rinds which are washed, or sometimes soaked, in a solution of brine or alcohol to add flavor and facilitate ripening, which takes place in humid cellars. Their rinds are usually quite shiny and vividly colored: the degree of apricot or red shading is determined by the duration and frequency of the washings. These cheeses do not sustain mold growth but their sticky surfaces attract cultures known as *bacterium linens* which aid development. Although they tend to be quite pungent—especially in hot weather—only the rinds smell (this is the reason they are seldom eaten); the interior cheese may be quite deliciously mild. Some cheeses, however, have pronounced aromas and are definitely an acquired taste!

BERGUES
A low-fat, brine- and beer-washed cheese from the Flanders province of northern France. Bergues is made from skimmed cow's milk and has only 15 to 20% fat. Because of this, it is ideal for dieters and a good keeper provided it does not dry out. Essentially a domestic cheese, Bergues is made by housewives and on small farms in either thick discs or flattened balls, 6-1/2 to 8 inches in diameter and 1-1/2 to 2 inches in depth. Curing takes place in humid cellars over a period of about two months. When ripe, the cheese has a smooth supple texture and mild flavor, with a hint of sharpness.

CHAUMONT
A small, cone-shaped cheese from Champagne with a depression at the top in which a puddle of brine collects during its two month curing spell. This seeps gradually into the cheese and produces a pronounced smell and robust spicy flavor. Chaumont's rind is very deeply colored, ranging from brick-red to a deep red-brown. A whole Chaumont weighs around 7 ounces and should be supple, never soft, to the touch. It is at its best when made in spring and summer from milk from pasture-fed cows.

COEUR D'ARRAS
As the name tells you, this strongly flavored, full-cream cow's milk cheese from Picardy is made in the shape of a heart. Like its close relation, Maroilles, it is washed in beer which gives it its striking red-brown rind. It has a soft supple interior.

DAUPHIN
Another relative of Maroilles, this crescent-, heart- or shield-shaped cheese is flavored with tarragon and pepper. According to legend, it was named after the son of Louis XIV who, while visiting the French Hainaut province, was served a flavored Maroilles which he greatly enjoyed. A dauphin weighs 7 to 18 ounces, depending on the cheesemaker, and is always about 1-1/2 to 2 inches thick. It has a smooth brown rind, fairly supple consistency and a rather overwhelming aroma. Again, it is at its best when made in spring and summer from milk from pasture-fed cows.

EPOISSES
A spicy, tangy, disc-shaped cheese from Burgundy which is washed in Burgundy *marc*. It has a strong bouquet and moist supple texture which ripens to the point of liquefaction. It is sometimes wrapped in paper leaves. Made from late spring and summer pasture milk, it has a three-month curing period.

ESROM
A semisoft, full-cream Danish cheese, formerly known as Danish Port-du-Salut. It has a creamy-yellow interior with many small, irregular holes and slashes. Rich and quite sweet when young, the cheese becomes much spicier and considerably stronger as it ages.

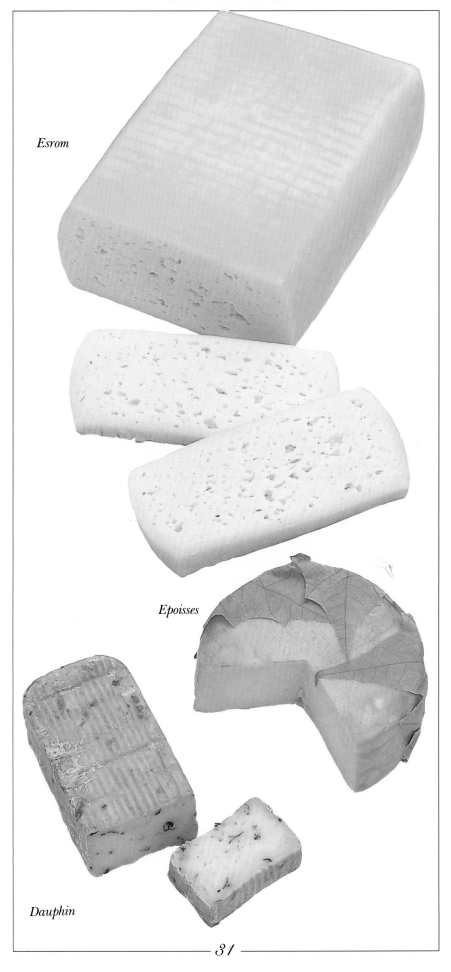

Esrom

Epoisses

Dauphin

Langres

LANGRES
A soft cheese shaped rather like a Yorkshire pudding with a concave surface to collect brine during washings, which later diffuses into the cheese. It ripens to a rich deep flavor and creamier texture than most brine-washed cheeses. Langres has an apricot-brown rind and a wonderful spicy bouquet. It is made in the Champagne region and a whole cheese weighs 9 to 11 ounces.

LIMBURGER
A cheese of Belgian origin now also made in Germany and Holland. Made from cow's milk, it has a fat content of 30 to 40% (slightly lower than average). Thought to be a monastic invention dating from the Middle Ages, it is brick-shaped with an appropriately colored brick-red rind. Pungent and spicy in both flavor and aroma, its fine-textured yellow interior tends towards suppleness.

LIVAROT
Made in the Normandy town of the same name, Livarot is thought to be a direct descendant of the Angelots of the past and was almost certainly invented by monks living in the region. It is sometimes called Livarot Colonel or the five-striper, a reference to the five bands of sedge which are traditionally used to hold it in shape. Nowadays, orange paper is often used in place of sedge. At its best from autumn to late spring, Livarot is a strong, spicy cheese, though rather less so than its bouquet suggests. It

comes in the form of a small glossy brown cylinder 5 inches in diameter, 2 inches in depth and weighing 12 to 16 ounces. Its interior should be smooth and its texture resilient.

MAROILLES
A solid, reddish brown, block-shaped cheese which was invented more than a thousand years ago by the monks of the Abbey of Maroilles. It is the oldest, best-known and most popular cheese of northern France. It is affectionately referred to as *le vieux puant* (the old stinker) in its home territory. While strong in flavor, it is by no means overpowering—the beer-washed rind is, again, the culprit. Its texture should be moist, not slimy, with few apertures in the cheese. A contrasting fine white line running through the center of the cheese is a good indication of ripeness.

MILLEENS
An Irish washed-rind, cow's milk cheese made solely at Eyries Farm, Bantry Bay, County Cork. It is a newly established cheese, invented by philosopher Veronica Steele to utilize surplus milk supplies. Milleens owes much of its character to the natural bacteria which flourish in the ozone-rich atmosphere of this coastal area and which lend the finished cheese its sweet pungent flavor and moist creamy texture. A fairly large disc-shaped cheese, Milleens is at its best during the winter months when it ripens uniformly beneath its orange-yellow rind.

Milleens

Livarot

Limburger

Maroilles

MUNSTER

An extremely popular cheese in Germany, Munster has been made in the Alsace region since the Middle Ages; both French and German varieties are produced. Munster is normally made in large disc shapes, about 8 inches in diameter and 2 inches thick. It is distinguished by its apricot-hued rind and semisoft interior which is straw-yellow in color. Smaller cheeses, 4 inches in diameter, are also made.

The two principal types of this cheese are **Munster Fermier** and **Munster Laitier;** the former is made by farms from unpasteurized cow's milk, the latter by commercial creameries from pasteurized milk. The fermier cheese is seasonal to summer and autumn, while the laitier is of consistent quality all year around. Brine-washed, Munster has a smooth red-tinged rind, searing bouquet and extremely spicy, tangy flavor. A caraway seed-spiced variety is also made.

MUROL

A pretty pink ring-shaped cheese from the Auvergne province of France, made from pasteurized cow's milk and washed with brine. The cattle in this region are grazed on mountain pastures which are inaccessible during the winter months, making the cheese available only during summer and autumn. Cured for a mere six weeks, Murol has a bland inoffensive aroma and mild succulent flavor. It is quite supple in texture.

NANTAIS

Also known as Curé de Nantes, this is Brittany's most celebrated cheese. Invented by a Breton parish priest in the 19th century, it is made from cow's milk in small factories. Nantais comes in the form of a square with rounded corners, about 3 inches square and 2 inches thick. Its brine-washed rind varies from straw-yellow to deep ochre in color, and it has a firm springy consistency and robust flavor. Though Nantais can be rather difficult to track down outside France, it is exported and well-worth searching for.

PONT L'EVEQUE

Made almost exclusively on farms in Normandy from rich milk from the sea coast, this is one of the oldest cheeses of the region; it was first recorded in the 13th century. A small, parallel-piped cheese with a dependable square base, it can be beige or orange in color but should always be supple. The interior has a very soft texture and is pale yellow in color. It has a pleasingly full-bodied flavor, with plenty of tang. Never buy Pont L'Evêque if it is runny.

REBLOCHON

A succulent farmhouse cheese from France's Haute Savoie *département*, Reblochon is the region's best-loved cheese—justifiably so, as it has a creamy, slightly aerated texture and a mild tangy flavor with background notes of nuts. Its crust can be either pale gold, apricot or deep orange: darker crusts indicate a stronger cheese. Consistency varies from firm to quite soft, particularly in summer when the cheese reaches peak condition; it remains there until early autumn.

REMOUDOU

Sometimes called Piquant, this is a Belgian cheese made from cow's milk in and around Liège by commercial dairies. Remoudou comes in trademarked, paper-wrapped cubes of about 3 inches, each weighing approximately 1-1/2 pounds. Its glossy, red-brown rind contains a powerful spicy cheese with lots of character and a very pungent aroma.

Munster

Reblochon

Murol

Nantais

Pont L' Evêque

SAINT-FLORENTIN

A soft farmhouse cheese from the Burgundy province of France, Saint-Florentin is made from whole cow's milk and is washed with brine during its two-month curing period. Made in the form of a flat disc about 5 inches in diameter and 1 inch thick, it has a smooth, shiny, red-brown rind and strong, spicy flavor with quite a noticeable tang. It is at its best from late spring until the end of autumn.

SAINT-NECTAIRE

A semisoft, lightly brine-washed cheese from the Auverge, Saint-Nectaire has been made since Roman times. It is made from mountain milk, redolent with the flavors and scents of alpine flowers and grasses. A mild, creamy cheese, it has a gentle tangy flavor and fragrant sweetness concentrated in its attractive red and mimosa-pigmented crust.

Saint-Nectaire is made in the shape of a disc, 10 inches thick. Pasteurized Saint-Nectaire has a rectangular green plaque in its center, the unpasteurized cheese has an oval one. Because it is made with milk from cattle grazed on alpine pasture, it is strictly seasonal and at its best mid-summer until the end of autumn. Saint-Nectaire is a distinctive, highly regarded cheese.

SAINT-PAULIN

An uncooked, pressed French brine-washed cheese made by commercial plants from pasteurized whole cow's milk. The cheese has a smooth, thin orange rind and homogeneous, pale cream interior. Its mild delicate flavor is enhanced as the cheese ages, becoming quite tangy.

The cheese is best known abroad under the brand name Port Salut, though the original Saint-Paulin was in fact an ancient, monastic cheese. The cheese is cured for around two months and made in the form of a small, thick dinner plate. It is highly versatile but does not lend itself well to cooking.

SAINT-REMY

A small Munster-type cheese made in the Lorraine province of France. A square block-shaped cheese which weighs around 8 ounces, it is cured with brine washings for six weeks. It has a smooth, light red-brown rind, penetrating aroma and medium strength, spicy flavor. Made by local factories, Saint-Remy is best avoided during the winter months when it will be made from inferior quality milk.

SORBAIS

A Maroilles-style cheese from Flanders, Sorbais is just a shade milder. Made from whole cow's milk in slabs weighing around 1-1/2 pounds, it is ripened for three months. Its rind is smooth, shiny and reddish brown, with a strong, fruity bouquet and encloses a soft, yet supple interior. Like Maroilles, this cheese is often used locally to make a special kind of cheese tart, called *goyère,* and when cooked, the flavor of Sorbais becomes suprisingly mild.

Saint-Nectaire

Saint-Paulin

Saint-Remy

Taleggio

TALEGGIO

Modern Taleggio is often a soft, bloomy-rinded cheese which bears no resemblance to the brine-washed original still made in Valsassina, a high, forested plateau in the Italian Alps. This has a strong, gutsy flavor redolent of sweet pasture. Made in 8-inch squares, 2 inches deep, Taleggio has a thin pink or straw-colored rind and ivory-hued, buttery interior.

TORVILLE

Made in England near Glastonbury Tor, which is reputedly the historical site of King Arthur's Camelot, Torville is actually Caerphilly washed with local Kneecracker cider. It is the Somerset pasture, however, rather than alcohol, which determines the nature of the finished cheese—sweet and fruity with an agreeable pungency. Torville is soft and creamy in consistency, but easily sliced. The rind is a dull orange shade.

TRAPPISTE DE BELVAL

A chunky, thick disc-shaped cheese about 10 inches in diameter and 5 pounds in weight, Trappiste de Belval is, by virtue of its size, an excellent cheese for keeping; it is brine-washed. A smaller 13-ounce version called **Dit D'Hesdin** is also made; this is washed in white wine. Trappiste de Belval is recognized by its pale apricot-hued rind, embossed with the marks of the jute cloth in which the cheese is wrapped before pressing. Properly matured specimens have girth rather than height and are moist, supple and agreeably mild.

VACHERIN

A generic name which covers a whole group of washed rind cheeses, hailing from the alpine regions of France or Switzerland. Vacherins are almost always larger than other washed rind cheeses; the smaller discs may weigh as little as 1 pound, but the larger wheels can tip the scales at 22 pounds. Production is by farms, dairies or picturesque chalets perched high in the mountains.

To categorize broadly, the larger cheeses are more supple than the tender, almost runny smaller ones. The color of their rinds also varies within the paler shades of the spectrum. All are brine-washed and made from full-fat cow's milk. Larger cheeses are usually more predictable in quality.

Trappiste de Belval

Torville

Blue Cheeses

Blue cheeses, with their attractive, mold-veined appearance and creamy-white interiors, are prized for their complex, piquant characters. The vast majority of blue cheeses are made from cow's milk, some, including Roquefort—the king of French blues—from sheep's milk and others from goat's milk. They are sold either with a natural, dry rind, or with the rind pared away, in which case they are foil-wrapped to prevent dehydration.

They are uncooked, usually unpressed (though some are lightly pressed) and made from crumbled curds which have been sprinkled with *penicillium glaucum*. Once formed, the cheeses are perforated with wire needles to allow aerobic development of the mold veins through the cheeses, within the humid, natural bacteria-rich cellars in which they are cured.

Without exception, blue cheeses ripen from the center to the crust and an even distribution of veins throughout is desirable. They are classed as soft cheeses and are characterized by their tangy, strong flavor and pungent aroma. However the strength of these cheeses varies considerably: not all are as strong as might be expected.

BEENLEIGH BLUE
One of the new breed of English farmhouse cheeses, Beenleigh Blue is made in Devon from the unpasteurized milk of Dorset/Friesland cross ewes. Since ewes, unlike cows, have only a six-month lactation period and the cheese takes approximately seven months to mature, it is available only from mid-autumn to late spring.

At the beginning of the season, Beenleigh Blue has a pure white interior with light blue-green veining and is quite mild and firm. As the cheese ripens further, it becomes creamier with a more pronounced flavor. The cheese has a natural skin, and is wrapped in paper. It normally weighs around 5 pounds.

BLEU D'AUVERGNE
A semisoft cow's milk cheese from the Auvergne province of France, made both on small farms and by commercial dairies. Based on a traditional Roquefort recipe, the interior is pale yellow and quite sweet with an even distribution of sharply flavored dark blue veins. The cheese is slightly greasy to the touch, has a powerful aroma and can sometimes tend towards saltiness. Again, it is made in 5-pound drums, which are foil-wrapped.

BLEU DE BRESSE
Often abbreviated to Bresse Bleu, this creamy soft cheese from the Pays de l'Ain is commercially produced from pasteurized cow's milk. Made in a variety of sizes in the shape of a cylinder, it is fairly richly flavored and not dissimilar to a Dolcelatte. It is usually foil-wrapped.

BLEU DES CAUSSES
An open-textured, penetratingly veined cheese with a delicious, concentrated creaminess. It is made in Roquefort country by commercial dairies, mainly from unpasteurized cow's milk, in 5-pound drums. Its best seasons are summer and autumn, when the cheese has been made from rich, fragrant summer pasture milk. The foil wrapper on every cheese bears a quality control label, guaranteeing its pedigree.

BLEU DE GEX
Thought by many experts to be one of France's most interesting blues, this natural-rinded, slightly pressed cheese is only rarely obtainable outside its native Pays de Gex and should be purchased immediately if sighted. Made by small farms and traditional dairies from full-fat, unpasteurized cow's milk, its unique delicate flavor is redolent of alpine flowers—the cows graze on high pastures above 6,000 feet. A flat, disc-shaped cheese with convex sides, it weighs 11 to 13 pounds.

Bleu des Causses

Bleu d'Auvergne

Bleu de Bresse

Bleu de Sassenage

BLEU DE SASSENAGE
A traditional, French, cow's milk cheese made in the Dauphine. It has a 45% fat content and a smooth natural rind. It takes three months to cure and reaches peak condition in summer and autumn when made from pasture milk. Similar in size to Bleu de Gex, it has a supple fine-grained texture and lightly colored, well-distributed veins. The flavor is slightly sharp and bitter.

BLUE BRIE
A commercially created soft blue cheese which is something of a phenomenon, as it has a bloomy white rind which is free of blue molds and therefore almost certainly sprayed on. Ripened cow's milk is innoculated with *penicillium* molds, then pierced to encourage development. The predominantly white interior resembles ordinary brie in texture but is slightly thicker. In flavor, Blue Brie is mild and rather bland, making it popular with hesitant blue eaters.

BLUE CHESHIRE
The original English Blue Cheshire came about by accident when mold developed in standard Cheshire cheeses. These rarities were known as Green Fades. Today, the molds are deliberately introduced and con-sequently the cheeses are much faster developing with a better distribution of veins. A full-fat, lightly pressed cheese (too much pressure would inhibit the flow of oxygen to the veins) with a thick, craggy, natural crust, blue Cheshire has a superb balance of strength and richness with nutty background notes. The veins are a dark green-blue, contrasting with the deep yellow, annatto-dyed interior. It is a considerably stronger cheese than ordinary Cheshire.

Two closely related cheeses are **Trinity,** which is harder in texture and deeper in color, and **Shropshire Blue** which has a more rugged looking rind.

BLUE VINNY
Once a popular English cheese made from partially skimmed milk, Blue Vinny disappeared from the market in 1982, though inferior Stiltons often tried to pass themselves off as such. Genuine Dorset Vinny, however, had to be made and ripened in the tack room of a stable to attract the bacteria necessary for its unique character. One Dorset farm is now producing the real thing again, but supplies of the 10-pound tubby, drum-shaped cheese are limited. It is a firm cheese with strong dark veining, which can taste rather dull.

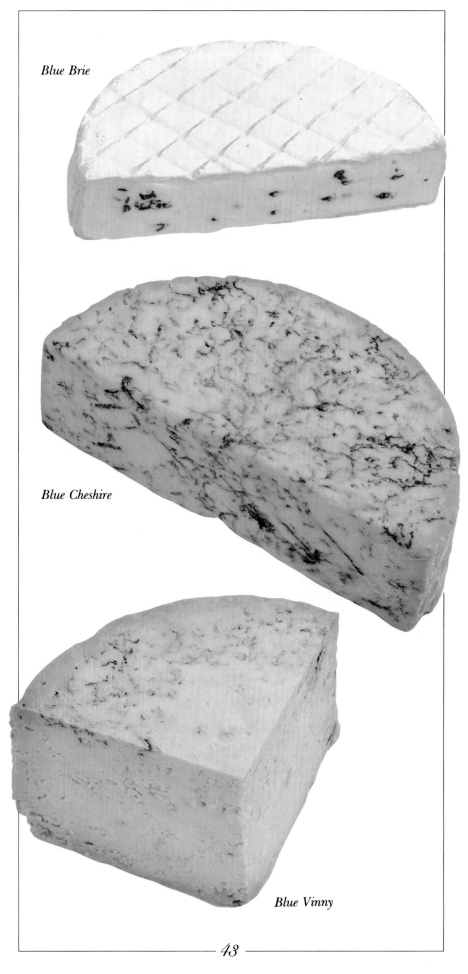

Blue Brie

Blue Cheshire

Blue Vinny

Blue Wensleydale

BLUE WENSLEYDALE
A semihard, cow's milk English cheese which is similar to Stilton but less creamy and crumbly. This cheese has been made since the 12th century, though not in its present form until the beginning of this century: prior to that it was almost entirely blue. During the Second World War, local production ceased, to be re-established later in the neighboring county of Derbyshire. Now it is once again made in the Wensleydale area.

CAMBAZOLA
A blue Brie-type German cheese of fairly recent invention. Like Blue Brie, it is entirely factory-made with synthetically produced molds and a white, sprayed-on bloomy rind. The interior is creamy white and soft with delicate blue-green veining. It is made in dinner plate-size wheels with a portion-marked foil wrapper.

CASHEL BLUE
A modern Irish cheese which combines the sweetness of a Gorgonzola with the pungency of a raw milk Stilton and the creaminess of a Roquefort. It is, however, loosely based on the recipe for a German blue cheese, Edelpizkase. Made in 3-pound foil-wrapped drums from unpasteurized cow's milk, it ripens in around two months. When mature, Cashel Blue has a thin supple rind, creamy pink-tinged interior (the pink is due to endemic local molds) and well-distributed blue-grey veins.

DANISH BLUE
This cheese was invented by Marius Boel, a Danish cheesemaker, early this century. He introduced a bread mold to a high-fat cheese and so created Danish Blue, now so popular that it is widely imitated worldwide. It has a stark, white interior with aggressive blue-black veining and a strong, bitter, salty flavor. It is made from pasteurized homogenized cow's milk and is foil-wrapped.

DORSET BLUE
A full-fat Stilton-type English cheese once widely made in the Dorset area, but production now is confined to a single farm in Sturminster Newton. Made from unpasteurized cow's milk, its scarcity adds to its value.

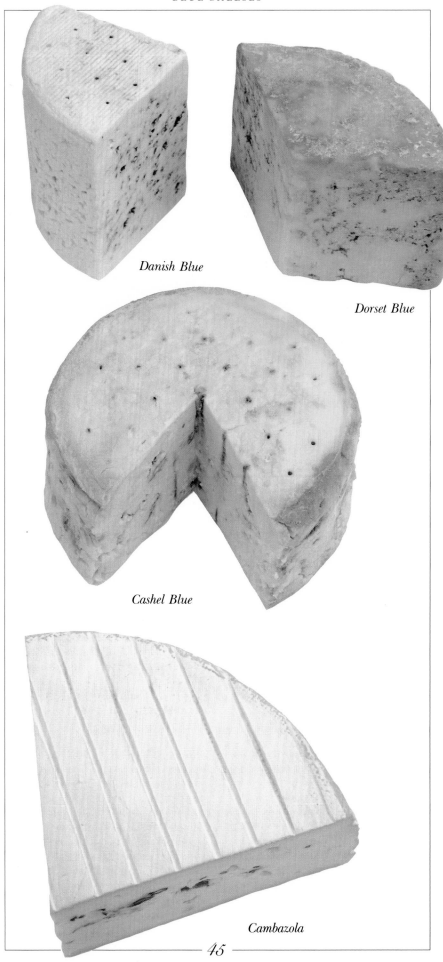

Danish Blue

Dorset Blue

Cashel Blue

Cambazola

Fourme d'Ambert

FOURME D'AMBERT
This cheese takes its name from the Latin noun *forma,* which describes its cylindrical shape. A full-fat cow's milk cheese, it is one of the rare French blues to have a crust. It is a very old-established cheese, known to have been made since the seventh century, and is as highly regarded by gourmets as Roquefort. Fourme is made by farms and small dairies and at its best is extremely creamy, nutty and full-bodied. Though quite supple, it should have plenty of give. Its best seasons are summer and autumn.

FOURME DE MONTBRISON
An almost identical cheese to Fourme D'Ambert in all respects, including its natural, dark grey rind. The main difference is origin: this cheese comes from the Forez province. Its prime seasons are also summer and autumn, when it is made from the best quality milk.

GORGONZOLA
This popular, well-known Italian cheese holds the distinction of being the oldest named cheese in the world: its first recorded mention was in AD 879. The town of Gorgonzola, after which it is named, was an established resting point for cattle on their annual winter drive from the alpine pastures to the stalls and this abundance of milk, together with the mold-rich local caves, united to produce excellent cheese. Unlike most blues, where even veining is desirable, Gorgonzola should have a greater concentration of molds towards the center of the cheese. This is because two days' curds with conflicting acidities and consequently poor homogeneity are used. Only one company now makes Gorgonzola according to traditional methods: the commercially made cheeses are invariably *dolce* (soft, sweet and like a Dolcelatte), not *piccante* (firm, heavily blued with a strong, spicy flavor) as the original.

HARBOURNE BLUE
A limited production, quite superb, goat's milk English blue from the same maker as Beenleigh Blue. Named after the Devonshire river close to where it is matured in a disused wine vat buried in the side of a valley, it has a firm yet creamy texture and full, goaty flavor. It is made in 5-pound foil-wrapped drums and is best kept refrigerated until just before serving.

LANARK BLUE
A recently established, hard sheep's milk cheese which is made in Scotland according to a traditional Roquefort-type recipe. Like all sheep's milk cheeses, it is seasonal, but sometimes the development of young cheese is artificially arrested by chilling to ensure year around availability. These adulterated cheeses should be avoided.

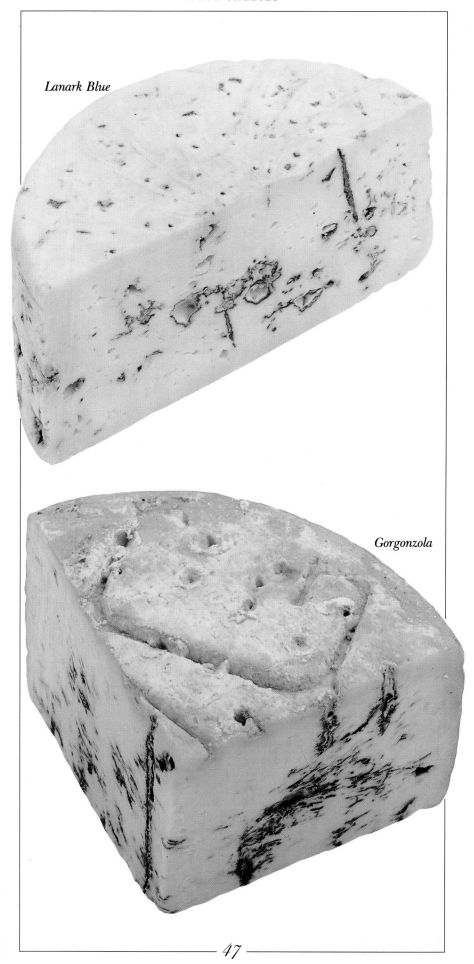

Lanark Blue

Gorgonzola

LYMESWOLD

A soft English cheese first made in Somerset in 1982 to utilize surplus milk. It is based on the German Bavaria Blau recipe. Like this cheese, it is lightly streaked with blue and has an artificially promoted bloomy white rind. When young, the cheese is quite supple with a mild delicate flavor which intensifies as it matures, developing distinct, tangy notes. Made in a Brie-shaped disc, it is usually foil-wrapped. Despite an extensive launch promotion, it has never really made a serious assault on the home market.

MYCELLA

A semisoft Danish cheese which is pale yellow in color with a deep green veining. The name is derived from the *mycelium* mold which lends the cheese its character. It has a pale brown crust and full Gorgonzola-like flavor.

ROQUEFORT

The most famous of all French blue cheeses, Roquefort's sublime nature fully deserves such renown. A very ancient cheese, it dates back to the time of the Gauls and was even mentioned by Pliny the elder in his Historia Naturalis. It was also a favorite of the Emperor Charlemagne, Charles VI and several popes.

According to experts, it owes its popularity not to the creamy, concentrated, unpasteurized sheep's milk from which it is made, nor to the *penicillium roqueforti* molds (also present in many other cheeses), but rather to the enormous limestone caves (called *cabanes)* in which it is matured. During the three months that the cheeses are cured there, natural spores circulate freely and aid their development.

Smooth, firm and buttery textured, Roquefort has a strong, well-rounded flavor and a faint moldy aroma. Roquefort is protected by strict government legislation so it tends to be of consistently good quality. However, like all the milk cheeses, it should be avoided during the spring months when it is almost certain to have been unnaturally preserved. The foil wrapper which protects its skin should be removed only immediately before serving to prevent dehydration.

SAINGORLON

A French-made blue cheese which is an exact imitation of Gorgonzola. Acceptable if the real thing proves difficult to come by.

STILTON

If Roquefort is the King of French blues, then Stilton has a justifiable claim to the English crown. As befits royalty, it has a bodyguard in the form of an association which protects its trademark. Although it originated in the Cambridgeshire town of the same name, now the only counties permitted to produce the *bona fide* article are Leicestershire, Nottinghamshire and Derbyshire. All manufacturers use whole, British cow's milk but only one, the Colston Bassett Dairy in Nottingham, uses unpasteurized milk.

A semihard cheese, Stilton is unpressed—hence its velvety, smooth texture—and has a thick, natural crust. The interior should be cream colored, never white, and spread with green-blue veins. Young Stilton has a mild, sharp quality which, when aged, gives way to a pronounced, full flavor. Stilton should never be scooped or macerated in port: both practices do the cheese a great disservice.

WHARFEDALE BLUE

A hard blue cheese from Yorkshire made from goat's milk. It is square in shape, weighs around 3 to 4 pounds and is finished with yellow wax to prevent moisture loss. Fairly mild when young, it has a powerful, well-developed flavor when fully mature. Wharfedale Blue is made in small quantities only.

WHITE STILTON

Included here because if kept long enough, White Stilton will eventually blue. It is firmer and milder than Blue Stilton and is a perfectly acceptable and refreshing alternative.

Roquefort

Stilton

White Stilton

Lymeswold

Uncooked Pressed Cheeses

This group encompasses a vast number of cheeses of greatly varying characters and textures. This variation is largely dependent upon the manufacturing process. In cheeses where the curd is transferred directly from ripening vat to weighted mold, the texture will be softer than in those whose curds are cut and milled to achieve a firm density. Obviously, this also affects the overall development of the cheese. All uncooked pressed cheeses have a natural rind, but in some cases this is scraped away and the cheese finished with wax to cut down on moisture loss. On those cheeses not treated thus, the marks of the cloth which lined the mold will often be clearly visible. Curing, which again varies enormously in duration, generally takes place in cool humid cellars.

ASIAGO

There are two varieties of this Italian mountain cheese from the Veneto. One, **Asiago de Allievo,** made in the mountain region of Vezzana from the unskimmed milk of cows grazed on summer pasture, is a seasonal hard cheese, at its best from mid-autumn to spring. The other, **Asiago Pressato,** is made from skimmed cow's milk and is an extremely close-textured, grainy cheese. When young it may be eaten sliced, but as it matures it becomes more suitable for grating. Made in medium-size wheels weighing 17-1/2 to 26-1/2 pounds, it has a yellow-beige interior and glossy, rich straw-colored rind.

BEAUMONT

Made in the Savoie province of France, Beaumont is distinguished by its tricolored red, white and blue paper wrapper. Made chiefly from unpasteurized cow's milk, it is at its best when made from spring and summer pasture milk. A whole cheese weighs around 3-1/2 pounds and has a regular, white-golden rind, close texture and supple, springy feel. Its creamy mild flavor is widely appreciated.

CAERPHILLY

This cheese takes its name from the Welsh village of Caerphilly. The creamy white, moist and crumbly cheese has a mild, salty flavor and a floury-white hard rind. It is said to be one of the most easily digested cheeses. Caerphilly closely resembles Wensleydale and like that cheese, it is particulary good served as a dessert, partnered with tart fruit pies.

CANTAL

A giant of a cheese from the Auvergne province of France, Cantal is made in drums approximately 18 inches in diameter and 16 inches high, each weighing 80 to 100 pounds. Sometimes called *Salers,* it is made from full-fat cow's milk and has a grey rind and creamy interior. Excellent as a table cheese, it is also valuable as a flavoring for cooked dishes such as soups, sauces and gratins. A semihard cheese, it comes in varying strengths from mild to strong. It is most versatile when creamy-tasting with background notes of nuts.

CASTLE HILL

A Cheddar-type cheese with a smooth firm texture and clean, sharp lingering flavor. Formerly a kitchen cheese (i.e., domestically made) it is now commercially produced in limited quantities. Two sizes are available: a 10-pound flat wheel and a 5-pound drum-shaped cheese. The smaller of the two is probably a better buy as it presses more satisfactorily, resulting in a closer texture, and matures more quickly. Made from unpasteurized cow's milk, Castle Hill is also suitable for vegetarians as it is made using non-animal rennet.

Castle Hill

Cantal

Asiago

Caerphilly

Cheddar

CHEDDAR

Indisputably England's most famous cheese, Cheddar is also its most widely imitated, using the original cheddaring technique devised in its native Somerset. The process involves cutting the curd repeatedly until a hot iron draws out a continuous elastic string when inserted. Once this is achieved, the whey is drained off and the curd cut with knives and stacked. This reduces its acidity levels and so stops the development of the cheese.

Nowadays, most Cheddar is made in blocks from pasteurized cow's milk, rather than from unpasteurized milk in the traditional drum-shape, and is sadly lacking in character. The best Cheddar is matured for a minimum of nine months, though often it is sold much younger than this. It should be neither crumbly nor rubbery in texture but smooth and firm. Color can be anything from pale ivory, through cream to annatto-dyed red. Mild, medium or mature, it is certainly one of the most versatile cheeses on the market.

CHESHIRE

The English Cheshire recipe has been exported worldwide, yet no other country has succeeded in reproducing the clean, acidic, nutty notes of this cheese, which are balanced by a meaty mellowness and moist, friable texture. A cow's milk cheese, made from both pasteurized and unpasteurized milk, Cheshire has a high acidity level which lends it its characteristically, flaky open texture. Now made almost entirely by factories, the only traditional Cheshire is made in Shropshire. Non-block Cheshires are made in large drums weighing 80 pounds or more and have a smooth, even rind verging on waxiness.

COTHERSTONE

One of the Dales' cheese, Cotherstone (pronounced Cutherstone) was created by French monks during the time of William the Conqueror. It is made with a mixture of milk from Channel Island and Friesland cattle and because of its high fat content, matures quickly. Left much longer than three to four weeks, it has a tendency to blue naturally. Made in the form of millstones, each 5-pound semisoft cheese has a natural crust which varies in color from pale apricot to deep, pink-gold, depending on the season, degree of ripeness and the surface molds. The cheese within is creamy in texture and pale gold in color.

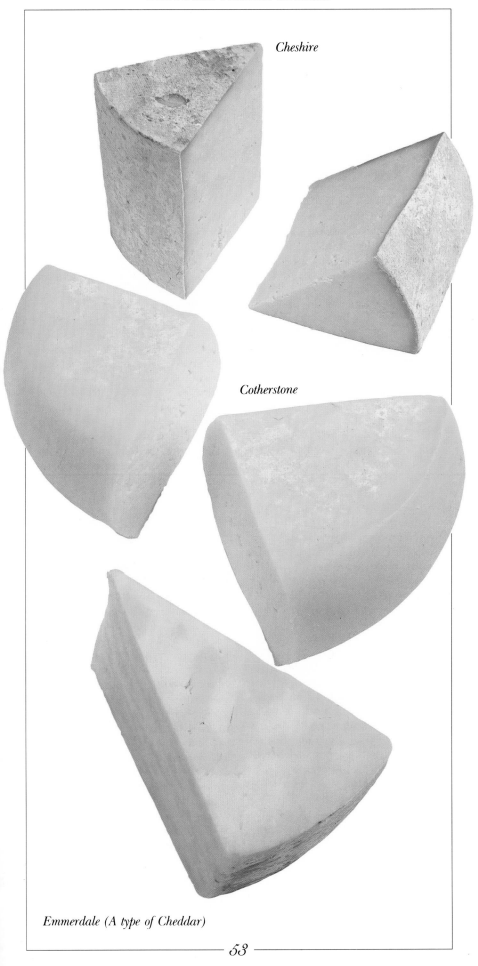

Cheshire

Cotherstone

Emmerdale (A type of Cheddar)

DERBY

One of the oldest-established of all British cheeses, Derby has affinities with both Cheddar and Cheshire but is somewhat softer in texture and more delicate in flavor than either. In its original form, this cow's milk cheese was made in drums about 15 inches in diameter and 5 inches deep, with a natural, wax-finished rind. Nowadays it is almost entirely made in rindless blocks and is relatively obscure. Better known is Sage Derby, a herb-flavored variant. This cheese has a waxy close texture with a fresh, green-marbled appearance and pronounced sage flavor, achieved by adding a liquid extract of the herb to the curds before molding and pressing.

EDAM

Dutch Edam is almost as well-known as Cheddar. It originates from the town of the same name. Similar to Gouda in taste, it is distinguished by being made from partly skimmed pasteurized cow's milk. The cheese has a fat content of 30 to 40%. It is manufactured entirely by factories in elongated 3- to 4-pound balls with red or yellow wax and has a smooth, supple waxy texture and sharp, slightly acidic flavor. It is much favored by dieters as it combines all the versatility of a hard cheese with the virtues of a reduced calorie content. It is also available flavored with cumin seeds or red peppers, in which case it has a brown-tinted rind.

EXMOOR

A Jersey milk, English Devonshire cheese of limited production which owes its origins to Wensleydale. Although made all the year around, winter cheeses are generally superior to those made during the summer months, being softer and creamier with a refreshingly sour-sweet flavor. Summer cheeses have a firm, flaky texture and a deep, buttercup-yellow interior. The cheese has a fairly thin natural crust, varying in color from golden brown to light grey.

FONTAL

A native of both France and Italy, Fontal is a full-fat cow's milk cheese made exclusively by commercial dairies. It is consistent in quality throughout the year and comes in the form of a flat cylindrical wheel about 15 inches in diameter and 24 pounds in weight. The cheese has a smooth, even, brushed rind, homogenous ivory-white interior and mild fruity flavor. A good cooking cheese, it is ideal in fondues and toasted cheese dishes.

FONTINA

Related to Fontal and similar in most respects, this long-established Piedmontese cheese was the gentry's choice as early as the 13th century. Unlike Fontal, however, it is made solely in alpine chalets in the Piedmont region of Italy and has a more obvious bouquet. Its ivory-yellow interior differs from Fontal, in that it is peppered with tiny holes. Fontina is a highly regarded Italian cheese, with a mild, yet distinctive flavor and a supple texture. Mature cheeses, with their firmer, drier texture, are particularly suitable when grated for use as a condiment.

GLOUCESTER (SINGLE)

This is the original Gloucester cheese—softer, milder and faster maturing than the ubiquitous Double Gloucester—with a fresh, light flavor. The cheese dates back to the eighth century when it was held in low esteem as a thin cheese, meaning one which is made from lower fat morning milk, or hay cheese, a reference to the fact that it was considered fit for consumption only by the harvest laborers. Genuine single Gloucester is made purely from the milk of Old Gloucester cows—not the higher yielding Friesans favored by commercial dairies. Only one maker, Charles Martell, produces the genuine article and his name has in recent years become synonymous with this cheese. Single Gloucester is best eaten at about ten weeks of age and benefits from the sap-filled zest of spring-pasture milk.

Exmoor

Edam

Fontal

Single Gloucester

Derby

Fontina

GLOUCESTER (DOUBLE)

A traditional English farmhouse cheese with a pale orange interior (it is colored with annatto) and a flavor which ranges from mellow and creamy to quite strong, depending upon the maturity of the cheese. The best Double Gloucesters are made from unpasteurized, full-cream, summer-pasture cow's milk. The adjective double refers to the fact that the traditional recipe for the cheese relied upon the milk from both morning and evening milkings. Such refinements are, however, largely ignored by the commercial dairies who make the block Double Gloucester which accounts for the bulk of the market. This cheese is slower to mature than Single Gloucester.

GOUDA

One of Holland's foremost cheeses, Gouda has been marketed for more than two hundred years. Most of the cheese that is exported is young cheese, no more than six weeks old. This is quite salty and dull in flavor, and can be recognized by its yellow-wax coating. Mature Gouda is an altogether superior cheese with a stronger, more pronounced flavor and a black-wax coating. The average weight of this flat wheel-shaped cheese is approximately 9 pounds, though both smaller and larger cheeses are available. Made from unpasteurized cow's milk, Gouda has a high butterfat content which contributes to its succulent creamy flavor.

HURSTONE

A descendant of the original Dunlop, which was a Scottish sweet or full-fat milk cheese. Like Dunlop, Hurstone is made from Jersey cow's milk which, with its high-fat content, makes this a rich creamy cheese. It is lightly pressed with a smooth close texture and comes in 5-pound and 10-pound drums. It reaches its peak at around three months old and its best season is autumn, when mature cheeses are redolent with the flavors of summer meadow herbs and flowers. Summer cheeses are also much deeper in color, owing to a high concentration of carotene in the milk. Although only limited quantities of this cheese are available, it does belong to the great tradition of British cheesemaking, which is currently enjoying a revival.

LANCASHIRE

Another traditional British farmhouse cheese which is now largely made in block form by commercial dairies. Authentic Lancashire has a very unusual and labor-intensive manufacturing process. Milk from both evening and morning milkings is ripened and the resulting curd hand broken, pressed and cut repeatedly within a short period. It is then combined with curd from the previous day, salted and milled before being transferred to molds and matured. Finished cheeses are waxed to prevent moisture loss. This rather long-winded procedure results in a cheese which is moist and flaky with an attractive, acidic flavor. As the cheese matures it becomes smoother and silkier, almost buttery, and correspondingly sweeter. Try it the way Lancastrians eat it—with slabs of fruitcake.

LEICESTER

Traditionally the name Leicester was synonymous with what we now know as Red Leicester: White Leicester came about as a result of a ban on food colorings during the Second World War and remained after this was lifted. A fairly hard-textured cheese, with an edible natural rind, it is made in commercial blocks of 20- and 40-pound drum shapes, noteworthy because at 20 inches across, they have the largest diameter of any English cheese. The flavor of Leicester is difficult to define when young, but as the cheese matures it develops a distinct nuttiness all of its own, which is complemented by its harder texture.

Double Gloucester

Leicester

Gouda

Lancashire

Leyden

LEYDEN

A Dutch cheese known as Leidsche Kaas in its homeland, this waxed rind, pressed cheese is made from full-fat cow's milk and flavored with caraway seeds. It is subjected to a two-pronged cure: first in humid cellars, then in a dry atmosphere. Made in the form of a flat cylinder with slightly convex sides, it has a firm supple texture and mild flavor enlivened by the caraway. A clove-flavored version of this cheese is also produced.

MIMOLETTE

Another Dutch cheese made from full-fat unpasteurized cow's milk. It is semisoft in texture with a rustic-looking even rind, dense, orange-colored interior (this is artificially colored) and pleasant nutty flavor. Each cheese weighs around 5 pounds and is shaped like a flattened ball. There is also a French version of this cheese, made in Flanders, which is practically identical.

PRESENT

A Dutch Gouda-style cheese which can be made from pasteurized or unpasteurized milk. It is similar to young Gouda in both taste and texture, being mild with a faint nutty background and firm supple consistency.

TOMME DE SAVOIE

Perhaps the best known of all the extended Tomme family, this deliciously mild cow's milk cheese has a fat content of only 20 to 40%. It has a firm, smooth yellow interior and hard, powdery natural crust which is predominantly grey but flecked with mimosa and red pigments.

Individual cheeses weigh 4 to 7 pounds and are cured for approximately two months: one month in cool humid cellars, followed by a month in a warmer environment to encourage the flavorful surface molds. In texture Tomme de Savoie is silky smooth and supple. This cheese is at its best during the winter.

WENSLEYDALE

Cheese was first made in the Wensleydale region during the Norman invasion, when French monks from the Roquefort region were brought over to Britian to practice their cheesemaking skills. Originally, like the cheeses after which they were fashioned, they were made from sheep's milk, but are now made from cow's milk exclusively by commercial dairies. A mild lightly salted cheese, Wensleydale has a crumbly, creamy-white interior and refreshing flavor. It is delicious served with fruit or even fruit pies, as is the local custom.

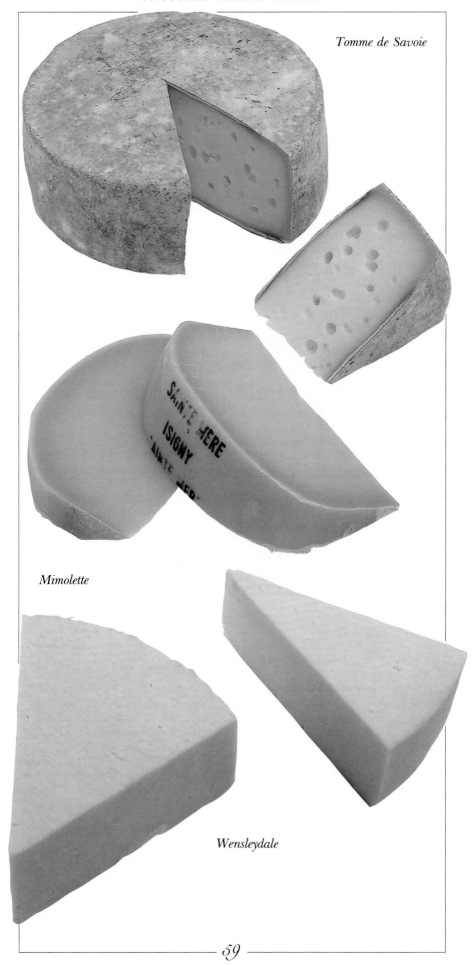

Tomme de Savoie

Mimolette

Wensleydale

Hard, Cooked Cheeses

Not necessarily always hard, but certainly always firm, these cheeses are said to be cooked, because the curd, after being broken up, is heated in the whey before being wrapped in cloth and transferred to the molds. The curd is then pressed down as far as possible to eliminate the maximum amount of moisture. This process subjects the cheese to a special fermentation which, during the course of ripening in warm cellars, makes it swell and develop apertures or holes. They are generally large cheeses, sometimes weighing more than 100 pounds with natural brushed and washed rinds.

APPENZELLER
Also known as Bloderkäse, this Swiss mountain cheese is made in alpine chalets from the milk of cows grazed high in the alpine pastures. Smaller than many cheeses of this type (each wheel weighs a mere 11 to 15 pounds) it is very firm in texture and its interior is dotted with perfectly formed pea-sized holes. Its rind is quite smooth. During its three to six month curing period, the cheese may be washed with herb- and spice-infused white wine or cider. Appenzeller has a pronounced fruity flavor and is ideal for cooking purposes.

BEAUFORT
Widely acknowledged to be the finest of the Gruyères, Beaufort is made in the Haute Savoie and Savoie *départements* of France, the milk from whose meadows lends the finished cheese a magnificient flowery-sweet, fruity flavor with a slightly salty tang. An *appellation d'origine contrôlée* cheese, this seal of approval guarantees that the cheese has been made and matured in the Savoie mountains for a minimum of four months. This is important, as the mountain caves are liberally endowed with *bacterium linens* which help to form the cheese's crust and so retain the moisture of the creamy smooth interior. Made in enormous wheels, a whole Beaufort weighs 90 to 130 pounds. The cheese is in quite short supply.

BITTO
From Lombardy in Italy, this rustic cheese has been produced in the same way for the past ten centuries. The cheese is made from a mixture of cow's and goat's milk. Fresh Bitto is ready in two months. The young cheese is pale and creamy but as it matures it develops a strong, aromatic flavor which closely resembles that of Parmesan.

COMTÉ
Another French member of the Gruyère family, its full name is actually Gruyère de Comté. Made from cow's milk in the mountainous Franche-Comté region since the 13th century, prime specimens have round marble-shaped holes. Comté has a stronger flavor than an Emmentaler: fruity and salty with a marked bouquet. Its rind is tough and darkly colored, enclosing a yellowish interior. Pleasant when eaten alone, it is also wonderful as an ingredient in a wide variety of cooked dishes: fondues, gratins, soufflés and sauces suggest themselves immediately.

EMMENTALER
A Swiss mountain cheese made from cow's milk and copied by other countries, notably France. The firm, thick, oily, golden interior has evenly distributed olive-shaped holes and a soft fruity flavor. Made in wheels which can weigh as much as 220 pounds, it is identifiable by the label of origin on the side of each cheese. According to French cheese expert Pierre Androuet, its size came about because of the necessity to store up dairy products over the alpine winters. Like Comté, Emmentaler is good as a table cheese and as an ingredient: in salads, canapés or sprinkled over soups and vegetables, or in cooked dishes.

Emmentaler

Comté

Beaufort

Appenzeller

FJORDLAND

A Norwegian cheese made from partially skimmed cow's milk. It has a pale smooth interior and unevenly distributed large round holes. It bears a passing resemblance to Emmentaler.

GRUYÈRE

First and foremost a Swiss national, Gruyère is now widely copied by other countries, including France and the United States. It is named after the village of its origin in the canton of Fribourg, where it is still made in the mountains. The cheese has a pale yellow, firm but friable interior, which is sparsely scattered with pea-sized holes. It has a rather sweet, fruity flavor, significant aroma and coarse reddish rind in which fine slits, known as *becs,* may be discerned. Wonderful both as a table cheese or a recipe ingredient.

HERRGARDSOST

One of the most popular of all Swedish cheeses Herrgardsost has been produced there since the turn of the century. A cow's milk cheese, its interior is medium firm and pliable with a sweet nutty flavor and a similar size and distribution of holes to Gruyère. The cheese is salted in brine then, about two weeks later, wax-finished. This makes it an extremely good keeper—it will show no sign of deterioration for at least a year. Like Gruyère, Comté and Emmentaler, this cheese melts easily when heated and consequently is suitable for use in cooked dishes.

JARLSBERG

An Emmentaler-type cheese from Norway with a pronounced, nutty flavor. It is made from full-cream cow's milk and has a golden yellow interior, slight sweetness and evenly distributed large holes. Once considerably cheaper than Emmentaler, its popularity has dispensed with its price advantage.

PARMESAN

Parmesan is the popular name of the best known of the *grana* family of Italian cheeses. Its correct name is Parmigiano Reggiano. This costly but rewarding cheese is made from skimmed cow's milk mixed with rennet and cooked for about 30 minutes, until the curds separate. The cheese comes in vast, shiny brown drums, weighing as much as 88 pounds, with the name stamped vertically all over the side. If the cheese bears no such identification, it is not the genuine article, although other similar cheese can be quite acceptable. Strict legislation controls its manufacture: it must be made between April 15th and November 11th.

A good Parmesan has a pale yellow interior with pin-head holes and a close-grained texture. When young and mild it is suitable for use as a table cheese. A whole Parmesan will keep for years, improving all the while. A cheese marked *vecchio* will have been matured for two years, one marked *stravecchio* for three years, and a *stravecchione* is an extra mature, four-year-old cheese. Young Parmesan will readily become hard, granular and grateable if stored in the refrigerator.

Parmesan is a basic ingredient of Italian cooking for the very good reason that it does not form threads as it melts. Grated, it is added to soups, sprinkled over pasta and rice, and used as a seasoning in vegetable and polenta dishes. It is also good on salads.

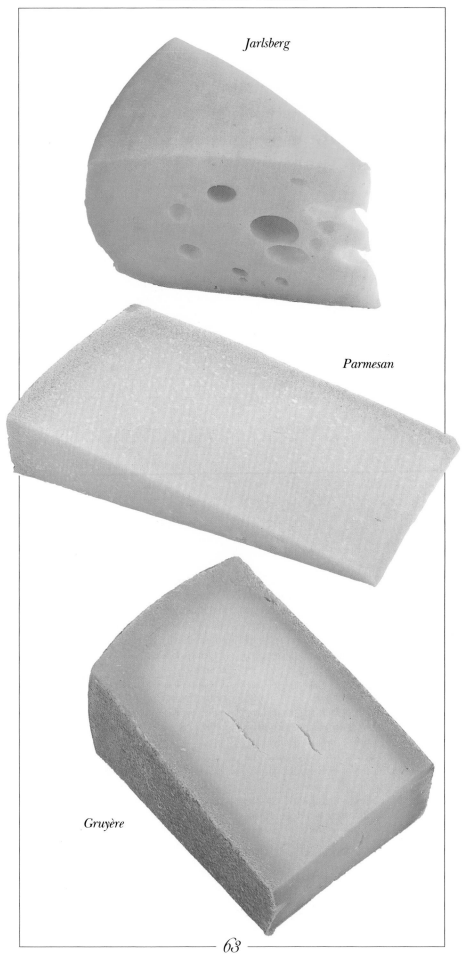

Jarlsberg

Parmesan

Gruyère

Samso

SAANEN
A very hard Swedish cheese with a brittle, deep yellow, hole-pitted interior. It is similar to Parmesan, having almost indefinite keeping qualities and, grated, may be used in much the same way.

SAMSO
An all-purpose, Danish, semihard, full-cream cow's milk cheese with a mild, sweet, nutty flavor when young. Mature cheeses are stronger and more pungent. The interior is pale yellow, with holes the size of cherries. As well as being an attractive dessert cheese, it lends itself well to cooking, particularly fondue and gratin-type dishes.

SAPSAGO
Made in Switzerland, Sapsago has many names, including Schabzieger and green cheese. It is virtually fat-free, being made from the reheated whey of skimmed cow's milk. A semihard cheese, it has a cylinder-like shape tapering towards the tip. Sapsago's flavor is strong and spicy and its texture is extremely hard, making it suitable only for grating. The unusual pale green color of this cheese is achieved by the addition of clover and powdered fenugreek. It is sold foil-wrapped, or powdered in cartons.

SBRINZ
Also known as *fromage à raper* (grating cheese), this Swiss full-fat cow's milk cheese has a dark yellow rind, dense yellow interior and brittle, hard texture. Seldom used as a table cheese, it is, like Parmesan, almost always used grated as a seasoning or recipe ingredient and was probably created to do away with the need to import Parmesan.

Sbrinz

Sapsago

Goat's Milk Cheeses

Goat's milk cheeses run a whole gamut of flavors, textures and types. Originally made in areas of poor pasture where only these hardy beasts could survive, they have become something of a cult and this has resulted in a large upsurge of numbers.

European goat's cheeses are invariably soft, depending on the way in which the curd is treated. They are not, strictly speaking, cured, but rather drained and allowed to dry out: for this reason it is perfectly possible to mature a fresh cheese at home provided suitable conditions exist.

Mature European goat's cheese have either a natural blue-mold rind, or a thick, white, artifically generated *penicillium* rind. Sometimes they are coated in charcoal ash *(cendre)*, flavored with herbs or wrapped in leaves.

While many producers of British goat's cheese follow the continent's lead, an increasing number base their recipes on traditional British hard cheese, lending them an altogether different character. Goat's milk cheese can be mild, subtle, sharp, brittle or just plain goaty—therefore they should always be approached with an open mind.

European goat's milk cheeses are invariably made from raw milk which results in a better quality, more interesting cheese.

Several goat cheeses are made in the United States. Usually quite good, most are available in the location where they are made.

BANON

A mild soft cheese from Provençe which is sometimes also made with sheep's or cow's milk. The goat's milk variety is at its best from late spring to early autumn. The cheese has a fat content of 45% and a natural rind attractively presented in a raffia-tied wrapper of chestnut leaves which have been marinated in *eau de vie*.

These parcels are left to ferment in terra cotta jars for a period of two weeks to two months, according to the desired degree of strength. They have a mild, nutty flavor, firm supple texture, sticky rind and faint dairy odor. An alternative version is made, known as **Banon au Pebre d'Ai,** which is flavored with summer savory.

BOUGON

This cheese from Poitou in France is similar in taste and texture to Bucheron but differs in appearance as it is molded into a flat, cylindrical shape. A soft cheese with a bloomy rind, it ripens in about two weeks and weighs about 9 ounces. It is usually sold boxed.

BUCHERON

A French cheese sometimes known as Bûche de Chèvre. The cheese has a thick, fluted white rind and is molded in the shape of a log.

CASTLE ASHBY

A medium-strength, semisoft English cheese made in Northampton. It is matured for just ten days, during which time it is coated with ash to form a soft, grey crust. The cheese is pyramid-shaped and weighs about 12 ounces.

CHABICHOU

A small, truncated cone-shaped cheese from Poitou, the stronghold of French goat's cheese production. A farmhouse cheese, Chabichou has a thin, blue, reddish-tinged rind, pronounced goat smell and a strong, sharp flavor. It takes three weeks to mature.

HALOUMI

A soft to semisoft Cypriot cheese which is salty, yet quite mild. It is generally served toasted and can be quite rubbery.

Bucheron

Banon

Chabichou

Haloumi

Bougon

Mendip Goat

MENDIP GOAT

A bulbous, thick-rind cheese which is part of the British cheesemaking revival, Mendip Goat is made in the west country from the milk of Anglo-Nubian and British Sannens goats. It has a sweet, complex flavor which really comes into its own when made from spring pasture milk. At that time of the year it has, according to one of Britain's foremost chefs, the aroma of truffles. One noteworthy feature of this cheese is the lattice indentations on its crust; these are caused by the plastic colanders in which it is molded. Mendip Goat takes approximately five months to mature and is available in limited quantities only.

MONTRACHET

A tall, cylindrical cheese from Burgundy, Montrachet is practically rindless. It is usually ripened in vine or chestnut leaves which should be removed before serving. Other versions are ash-covered, or coated with chopped herbs. Individual cheeses weigh about 3 ounces and take about ten days to ripen. Supple in consistency, this cheese has a faintly discernible goaty smell and mild creamy flavor.

MOTHAIS

Also known as Mothe-Sainte-Heray, this commercially made cheese comes plain or with a *cendré* coating. The former are disc-shaped, the latter pyramid-shaped: both weigh approximately 8 ounces. Tender rather than soft in texture, they are quite robustly flavored. They are from the Poitou province of France.

RIBBLESDALE

A lightly pressed, wax-finished English cheese made in north Yorkshire. It has a moist, semisoft texture, and delicate, lightly salted flavor. The cheese varies from season to season with the variations in protein and fat content of the milk. Winter cheeses are softer and creamier than their crumblier, summer and autumn counterparts. An oak-smoked version is also made.

SAINT-CHRISTOPHE

At its best from early spring until mid-autumn, Saint-Christophe comes from the Tourangeau region of France, where goat's milk cheeses are thought to have been first introduced by the Saracens back in the Middle Ages. A log *chèvre* with a natural rind, Saint-Christophe is modelled on the original log *chèvre*, Sainte-Maure. It has a deliciously creamy, succulent softness and perfectly balanced flavor when made from summer pasture milk. Saint-Christophe has the rustic finishing touch of a straw running through the interior to facilitate lifting during ripening.

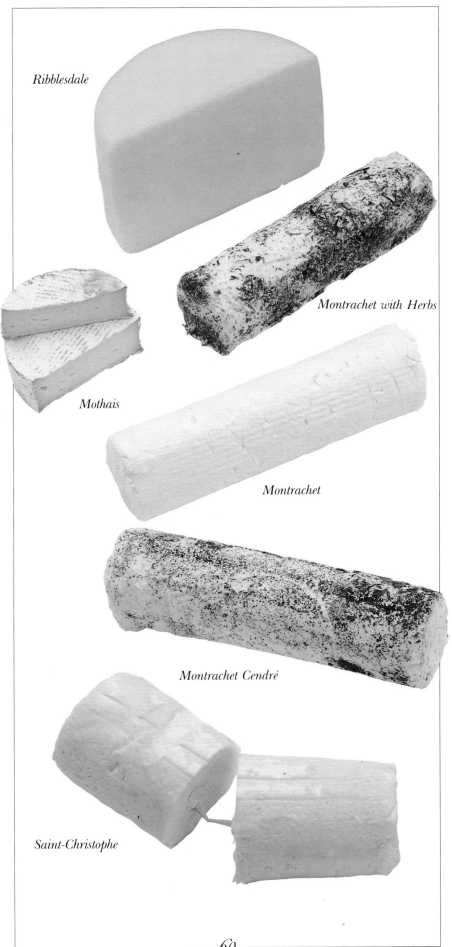

Ribblesdale

Montrachet with Herbs

Mothais

Montrachet

Montrachet Cendré

Saint-Christophe

Sainte-Maure

SAINT-MAURE

Also known as Chèvre Long, this log-shaped cheese from Touraine was originally produced solely on farms but is now made chiefly in factories. It has a bloomy, artifical rind, strong mold aroma and full goat flavor. Packaged in paper, in deference to its forebears, it is sometimes made with a straw running through its center. It has a firm but yielding texture which can develop graininess if improperly kept. It is cured in cool, dry cellars for approximately one month.

SATTERLEIGH

A Devonshire goat's cheese made on much the same lines as a Cheddar, Satterleigh is a firm, subtly flavored cheese which is at its best from late spring until early winter. A hard, pressed cheese, it is made in 4-pound drums and matured for approximately four months. As a young cheese it is white, but as it matures it develops a creamy complexion. Unlike many goat's cheeses, it is very stable and hard to mishandle.

TOMME DE L'ARDÈCHE MERIDIONALE

A traditional *chèvre* from the heart of the Ardèche, this is one of the oldest established and most consistently successful of all the *chèvre* family. Made in the form of flattish discs, each weighing about 13 ounces, these cheeses mature in about five weeks. Tomme de l'Ardèche Meridionale has a gently undulating crust im- printed with the marks of the straw mats on which it is matured and is delicately flecked with blue molds. It has a delightful fresh flavor, light texture and complex bouquet. Resist the impulse to remove its rind before eating, as many experts believe that the greatest flavor is concentrated there.

TYMSBORO

A soft mild cheese which is ready to eat after just two to three weeks maturation. This English cheese is made from unpasteurized goat's milk in the heart of Shakespeare country. It is either round or pyramid-shaped. Tymsboro is mold-ripened and therefore has a white, downy rind, generally flecked with blue.

VALENAY

Both creamery and farm versions of this cheese are made in the Poitou region. The creamery type has an artifically promoted bloomy rind, while the farm cheese is natural and charcoal-dusted. Both are an attractive pyramid shape and weigh approximately 10 ounces. The farm cheese is seasonal, at its best from spring to autumn when it has a deep, blue skin, firm yet tender consistency, delicate goat and mold aroma and mild, nutty flavor. The creamery version is available all year around (off season it is made from frozen curd). This cheese is contrastingly firm and supple with an intense aroma and undistinguished, salty flavor.

Valençay

Tymsboro

Tomme de L'Ardèche Meridionale

Sheep's Milk Cheeses

Creamy, white sheep's milk is a great deal more concentrated than that of either cows or goats. It has much higher levels of both fat and casein (an important substance for the formation of curd). It is ideally suited to both soft and hard cheesemaking processes and the resulting cheeses are rich and flavorsome regardless of their strength.

The chief drawback lies with the faster maturing cheeses: because ewe's lactate only between spring and autumn, they are unavailable during the winter. Some producers attempt to bridge the gap by freezing curd to be matured during the colder months, but this is largely unsuccessful as cheeses made from frozen curd never develop as well as their fresh curd counterparts. It is worth noting, however, that finished cheeses may be frozen without detriment, provided they are eaten on the day of thawing.

These cheeses deserve attention on their own merits but are also invaluable for those who suffer allergies to cow's milk cheeses yet find goat's milk cheeses too strong.

AMOU

A French, uncooked, pressed cheese from Gascony, made exclusively by farms. It has a natural golden-colored rind whose neat appearance is the result of frequent washings and oilings during its two to six month curing period. Depending on age, its texture may be firm and resilient or hard and crumbly; its flavor too, progresses from mild to quite sharp. Mature cheeses are better grated and used like Parmesan than eaten as they are. Amou is made in the shape of a thick disc and each cheese weighs approximately 10 pounds.

ANNOT

Sometimes referred to by its more formal title, Tomme d'Annot, goat's milk may sometimes be substituted for sheep's in its manufacture when supplies are short. Made by mountain farms in the Comté de Nice province of France, it is a disc-shaped, uncooked pressed cheese with a smooth pale rind. It has a mild, nutty flavor, supple texture and faint sheep aroma. Cured for about two months, it is at its best throughout the summer.

BARAC

A hard, Scottish cheese made in much the same way as the English Dales' cheeses, Barac is acknowledged by experts to be one of the best British sheep's cheeses in existence. It has a superb balance of sweetness and acidity and a soft, crumbly consistency when young. If matured for longer than the normal six to seven months, the flavor gains depth and the texture smoothness; color, too, deepens from pure white to cream. Only limited quantities of this excellent cheese are available.

FIORE SARDO

Also called Pecorino Sardo, this lightly pressed cheese from Sardinia has a natural white to yellow oiled rind, and fresh, nutty flavor which develops sharp, salty notes as the cheese matures. Soft as a young cheese, it hardens with age when it is best used grated, as a seasoning.

LARUNS

A semicooked pressed cheese from the Basque country, this cheese is made in the form of a flattened loaf about 12 inches in diameter, 3-1/2 inches deep and weighing about 12 pounds. It has a smooth, thin natural crust which varies in color between straw-yellow and ochre. It is cured in humid cellars for two to six months, according to whether it is destined for table or saucepan. After two months, it is tender yet supple with a mild, nutty flavor. Older cheeses are hard and brittle with a very strong, sharp flavor. It is essentially a domestic cheese.

Barac

Fiore Sardo

Sheviock

NIOLO

A soft, farmhouse cheese from Corsica with a natural, lightly brine-washed rind. It is made in a rounded square shape, imprinted with the marks of the basket in which it is molded, and each cheese weighs about 1-1/4 pounds. Its rind has a smooth, clean, greyish-white appearance and smells strongly of sheep. In mature cheeses, the interior is firm, buttery and sharply flavored with a full bouquet. Fresh, unripened cheeses are mild, creamy and oily-textured.

PECORINO ROMANO

A very ancient Italian, cooked, pressed cheese made in dairies around Rome. It has a somewhat lower fat content than most related cheese—only 36%. Made in medium-size cylindrical wheels, each weighing 13 to 26 pounds, it has a natural white to dark yellow rind (some cheeses are oiled using olive oil dregs tinted with ochre) and white to pale yellow interior. A densely textured cheese with a hint of smoke about its aroma, Pecorino Romano is aged for a minimum of eight months and is extremely strong. Younger cheeses are suitable for the table but mature specimens are best treated as aged Parmesans.

PECORINO SICILIANO

Also called *Canestrato,* after the baskets in which the curd is drained, this Sicilian cheese is uncooked and pressed and also differs from its Roman cousin in that it has a slightly higher fat content—usually more than 40%. Similar in size to Pecorino Romano, it is matured for half as long yet attains equal strength of character. It is something of an acquired taste, being fiercely sharp and almost rancid. It has a natural white to yellow oiled rind and a dense, white interior.

SHEVIOCK

A relatively new British cheese made with milk from British milk sheep and marinated in cider from its native Cornwall. It is made to a Cheddar recipe and has a smooth moist texture and subtle refreshing flavor. The drum-shaped cheese weighs about 4 pounds, has a good, natural crust and is made in limited amounts only.

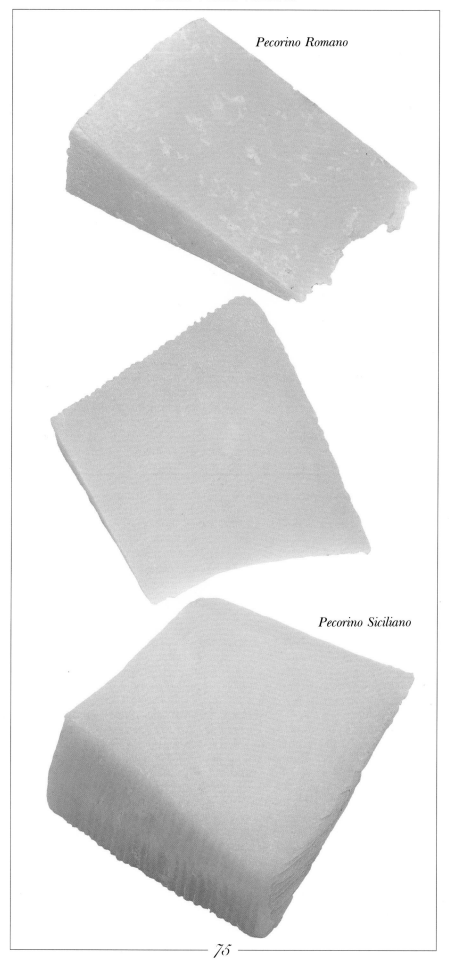

Pecorino Romano

Pecorino Siciliano

Spenwood

SPENWOOD

Another newly established British sheep's milk cheese of limited production and consistently high quality. It is made in wheels of approximately 5 pounds and has either a natural rind the color of cement or a waxed finish. In common with most sheep's milk cheese, Spenwood is at its best when made from spring pasture milk and its flavor benefits from its five months maturation. At this age it has a smooth, supple, slightly grainy texture and a mild flavor which is reminiscent of barley.

SARTENO

An uncooked, pressed cheese from Corsica with a filmy, pale yellow natural rind. Sarteno may be made from goat's milk or a combination of both sheep's and goat's milk. Made in the form of a flattened sphere of about 5 inches in diameter and 4 inches in depth, each cheese weighs 2 to 2-1/2 pounds and is matured for three months in dry cellar conditions. At this age it has a firm but not brittle texture, subtley penetrating aroma and strong sharp flavor. It is named after the principal market town in the southwest of the island and is thought to have been manufactured in this region since Roman times. Sarteno is best eaten young as a dessert cheese but more mature specimens may successfully be used grated, as a seasoning or garnish in much the same way as Parmesan.

TOMME DE BRACH

A soft sheep's milk cheese from the Massif Central region of France where it is made almost entirely on farms. It is best during spring and summer. Tomme de Brach has a smooth, natural rind and somewhat oily consistency. Cured in dry cellars for between two and three months, each small, drum-shaped cheese weighs about 1-1/2 pounds and is 4 inches in diameter. It has a fairly strong flavor and definite sheep aroma. The term *tomme* is simply a French dialect word for cheese; it does not refer to a specific cheese grouping.

TOMME DE CARMARGUE

Sometimes known as Tomme Arlesienne, this soft, fresh cheese originates from Provence. It is made by small dairies and is at its best during spring and winter. Mild and creamy, it is flavored with ground thyme and bay leaves. It has no rind, but a filmy pale ivory skin to which a bay leaf is banded. Tomme de Carmargue has a mild, creamy flavor, with a suggestion of herbs. It is usually molded in small squares of about 2-1/2 inches, and allowed to drain for 1 week. It can, if desired, be aged quite successfully. Like most tommes, it is difficult to find outside France.

Venaco

TOMME DE VALDEBLORE

An uncooked, pressed milk cheese from the Comté de Nice province of France, Tomme de Valdeblore is a mountain cheese which is sadly becoming increasingly scarce. Cured in dry cellars, with occasional bursts of humidity, for anything from three to six months, it has distinctive characteristics according to its age: young cheeses have a pinkish grey rind, tender but supple consistency, mild, creamy lactic taste and are virtually without aroma; mature cheeses have a grey-brown rind, hard texture (which retains some give), sharp flavor and pronounced sheep aroma. Locally, older cheeses are considered superior; elsewhere younger cheeses are preferred. Made in flat cylinders of 20 pounds or more, this cheese is closely related to Tomme d'Annot.

VENACO

A soft, Corsican mountain cheese which may also be made from goat's milk. It has a natural rind which is generally scraped away leaving a greyish white surface. The cheese is matured in humid rock caves for three to four months and has a firm oily texture, powerful fermented smell and pronounced, sharp sheep flavor. Venaco can be eaten as it is or, as Corsicans enjoy it, mashed and marinated in robust red wine.

Soft Cheeses with Natural Rind

This category of cheese falls somewhere between those with bloomy rinds and those with washed rinds. On the whole, they develop neither the softness of the first, nor the pungency of the latter. The ripening of such cheeses is double-edged: both from the interior to the rim and from the crust to the center. In a good, even-textured cheese, these two processes will have kept pace with each other. A number of cheeses in this group are coated with wood ash (cendré) during curing; this not only looks attractive but improves the flavor and keeping qualities.

BARBEREY

A Champenois cheese which is also known as *Fromage de Troyes* or *Troyen Cendré,* Barberey is made by small dairies using skimmed cow's milk and has a fat content of a mere 20 to 30%. Cured in wood ash for about a month, the cheese has a subtle musty aroma and rather sharp flavor. It is made in small discs, weighing about 9 ounces. Barberey is at its best during spring and autumn.

FRINAULT

A full-fat cow's milk cheese from Orléans in France, which is at its best when made from summer and autumn pasture milk. Named after its creator, it has a delicately colored, bluish rind, tender-soft texture and full flavor. It takes just three weeks to come of age because of its diminutive size: each whole, thin disc-shaped cheese weighs only 4 ounces. A *cendré* version is also made. Frinault is closely related to Olivet Bleu.

GUÉRET

A farmhouse cheese from the Marche province of France which also goes by the name of *Creusois* or *Coupi.* It is made from cow's milk which is almost completely skimmed to give a fat content as low as 10%. Guéret is an irregular disc-shaped cheese, about 5 inches in diameter and 1-1/2 inches deep. It is ripened in sealed terra cotta pots for up to six months, depending on conditions. The resulting cheese has an ultra-smooth, sticky rind, pronounced smell and quite mild flavor. In appearance, the interior is translucent. It is used as a dessert cheese or grated, sprinkled over local dishes.

HEILTZ LE MAURUPT

A rustic, ash-coated cheese made from partially skimmed cow's milk which is also known as *Cendré d' Argonnes.* Production is centered in the Champagne region of France and geared toward the hay and grape harvests when it is served to farm laborers. Dry-cured for two to three months, the cheese has a firm but yielding consistency, insignificant aroma and a strong, spicy flavor. Whole cheeses are Camembert-size but lighter, weighing only 10 to 12 ounces. Try serving this cheese instead of the usual Cheddar as the basis of a deliciously different ploughman's lunch.

MIGNOT

This full-fat cow's milk cheese from Normandy reaches prime condition during the autumn and winter. It is made entirely on farms and matured in humid cellars for one month. Firm and fruity with lots of bouquet, it has a red, oily natural rind and pale ivory interior. It comes in discs about 5 inches in diameter and 1-1/2 inches deep.

NOYERS LE VAL

Another harvest cheese which is made by farms in the Champagne region of France to sustain laborers during grape picking. The cheese is made from semiskimmed cow's milk with a fat content of 30 to 35% and is cured in ash in dry cellars for between two and three months. It is firm and quite supple in texture and though it has no aroma worth speaking of, this is more than compensated for by its strong, spicy soapy flavor. In appearance Noyers le Val is attractively rustic: an irregularly shaped disc which is liberally coated with ashes. Whole cheeses are about 5 inches in diameter, weighing 12 ounces.

Frinault

OLIVET BLEU

A traditional, dairy-made cheese from the Orléanais province of France. It is made from whole cow's milk and has a natural, blue, quite bloomy rind. It is cured in local chalk caves for approximately one month and sold *au naturel*, or wrapped in paper or plane tree leaves. Its season extends from spring to the end of autumn, during which time it has a smooth, straw-yellow interior, even, rich, supple texture and mild fruity flavor. It is made in the form of small, flat discs weighing about 11 ounces. A *cendré* version is also produced, which takes rather longer to reach maturity.

OLIVET CENDRÉ

Olivet Bleu's ash ripened relative, Olivet Cendré also hails from the Orléanais province of France. Like Olivet Bleu, it is made in traditional dairies from cow's milk but has a slightly lower fat content of around 40%. Because of its slower maturation period—three months as opposed to one—its season extends into the winter months. The two cheeses are practically identical in size, about 5 inches in diameter, though quite different in appearance and flavor. Olivet Cendré's distinctive grey ash coating contains a much more savory, firmer, full-bodied cheese. (Photograph on page 80.)

Olivet Cendré

PANNES CENDRÉ
This is the same type of cheese and from the same area as Olivet Cendré, the chief difference being that Pannes Cendré is made from skimmed cow's milk. A thick, handsomely shaped cheese, it has a supple texture, natural mold and strong flavor with soapy background notes.

RIGOTTE DE CONDRIEU
A full-fat cow's milk Lyonnaise cheese made entirely by small dairies and available all the year around. It has an annatto-tinted natural rind, so thin as to be barely discernible. Because of its minute size (whole cheeses are 1-1/2 inches in diameter and depth), it takes only two weeks to mature in dry conditions. It is quite a firm-textured cheese with an indistinct aroma and mild, occasionally lactic flavor.

RIGOTTE DE PELUSSIN
A traditional farmhouse cheese from the Auvergne, unusual in that it is made with a mixture of cow's and goat's milk. Rigotte de Pelussin is made in the form of a squat cone, a mere 1 inch in height and weighing only 3 to 3-1/2 ounces. Because of its tiny size, it ripens in a mere three weeks in dry cellar conditions, during which time it develops a delicate, blue-tinged rind and an appealing mild, nutty flavor. It should be firm in texture, never dry. Rigotte de Pelussin may also be made purely from goat's milk.

SAINT-MARCELLIN
According to French legend, this is the cheese that once sustained Louis XI after an ordeal involving a bear in the Forest of Lenta, close to where it is made. In those days, though, the cheese would almost certainly have been made from goat's milk; this was later combined with cow's milk and today it is made exclusively from the latter by farms and small dairies. A small, soft, supple cheese, it has a thin, apricot-colored rind which is flecked with delicate, blue-grey molds, a faint, lactic aroma and refreshingly sharp flavor. It is ripened first in humid caves, then later in ventilated drying rooms for a total of one month. Saint-Marcellin is about 3 inches in diameter, and weighs only 3-1/2 ounces.

Saint-Marcellin

Rigotte de Condrieu

Processed Cheeses

Just as commercially produced pasteurized cheeses can never compete with raw milk farm cheeses for their subtle nuances of flavor and amazing range of textures, processed cheeses are at a distinct disadvantage, being manufactured according to scientific formula rather than traditional recipes. Nonetheless, provided they are chosen with care some can be a welcome addition to the cheese board and they do have the virtue of keeping well, being of a more stable nature. A word of warning though: while it may be acceptable to serve a Roulé or a Tomme au Raisin, it is unforgiveable to offer a square of processed plastic in place of proper Cheddar.

AUSTRIAN SMOKED CHEESE

A medium-fat, sausage-shaped, lightly smoked cheese with a firm, rubbery texture. It is made from cow's milk and sold in wax-finished portions.

BEL PAESE

An Italian, foil-wrapped soft cheese with a buttery, spreadable texture which is often sold in individual portions. It has a mild, fruity flavor and appealing, lactic aroma and is ideal for sandwiches.

LAYERED CHEESE

There are many layered cheeses on the market. Huntsman is the brand name of one English cheese made by a dairy in Melton Mowbray, Leicestershire, and consists of a layer of Stilton sandwiched between two layers of Double Gloucester cheese. Numerous variations on this theme exist but unfortunately, and without exception, they look rather better than they taste.

ORANGERULLE

A full-fat soft, fresh, tube-shaped cheese which is flavored with Grand Marnier and rolled in hazelnuts. It is rather rich, but quite pleasant as a dessert.

ROULÉ

A soft, fresh cheese not dissimilar in texture to a *chèvre*, which is now widely available. The cheese is spread with either herbs and garlic or fruit and formed like a jellyroll. It is sold presliced and looks quite attractive.

TOMME AU NOIX

A soft bland cheese with an ivory white interior whose surface is studded with walnuts. The actual cheese was originally made in Savoie and ripened in caves but production has now shifted entirely to factories. The nuts are quite a pleasant foil to the smoothness and bland flavor of the cheese.

TOMME AU RAISIN

Sometimes also called *Fromage au Raisin*, like Tomme au Noix this cheese originated in the Savoie province of France where it was ripened in a mixture of grape skins, pulp and seeds. Nowadays, factory-produced cheeses are rolled in black grape seeds after manufacture and consequently they lend little to the flavor of the cheese. It is mild and quite fruity, with a chewy texture.

WINDSOR RED

A Cheddar-style cheese which is flavored and colored with elderberry wine; the Irish do the same thing with Guinness. Red Windsor has a crumbly texture and a flavor similar to mild Cheddar.

Tomme au Raisin

Bel Paese

Austrian Smoked

Tomme au Noix

Windsor Red

Huntsman

Roulé

Orangerulle

Danish Dip

2/3 cup half and half
2/3 cup dry white wine
2 egg yolks
4 ounces Danish blue cheese, coarsely
  crumbled
2 teaspoons finely chopped dill weed

To Garnish:
Dill sprigs

To Serve:
Selection of raw vegetables, including
  julienne strips of carrot, red and
  yellow bell peppers and zucchini;
  celery sticks; cauliflowerets; and
  blanched asparagus spears

In a bowl, blend together half and half and wine; immediately beat in egg yolks. Stir in cheese. Pour into the top section of a double boiler set over barely simmering water. Cook a few minutes, stirring constantly or until thick and smooth. Remove from heat and stir in dill weed. Let cool. Pour into a serving dish, cover and chill until required.

To serve, place the dish of cheese dip in the center of a serving platter, garnish with dill and surround with prepared vegetables.

Makes 1-1/4 cups.

Horseradish Dip

1/2 cup fromage frais or plain yogurt
4 teaspoons prepared horseradish
1/4 teaspoon ground pepper
1/4 teaspoon garlic salt

To Serve:
Pretzels
Poppadums
Cheese Straws (see note)

In a bowl, blend together all the ingredients. Cover and refrigerate 3 to 4 hours for the flavors to develop, then pour into a serving dish. Accompany with pretzels, poppadums and Cheese Straws.

Makes 2/3 cup.

Note: To make cheese straws, roll out some ready-made puff pastry on a lightly floured surface. Using a sharp knife, cut into finger-size rectangles. Brush with beaten egg and sprinkle with grated cheese and sesame, poppy or caraway seeds.

Put the pastry rectangles on a dampened baking sheet and bake in a preheated oven 400F (205C) about 10 minutes or until puffed and golden brown. Transfer the cheese straws to a wire rack to cool.

White Stilton & Leek Soup

3 leeks, about 12 ounces total, thinly
   sliced
1 small potato, diced
3 cups homemade chicken stock
4 ounces white Stilton cheese,
   crumbled
Pepper, to taste
2 tablespoons half and half

To Garnish:
Parsley sprigs or a few reserved leek
   rings

Put leeks into a large saucepan with potato and stock and cook about 20 minutes or until vegetables are soft.

Puree vegetables and stock in a blender or food processor fitted with the metal blade until smooth. Return soup to pan and add Stilton. Heat gently, stirring constantly or until cheese melts; season with pepper.

Divide soup among individual bowls and spoon over a little cream. Create a feathered effect using a wooden pick or a small skewer. Garnish each portion with parsley sprigs, or leek rings (see note).

Makes 4 to 6 servings.

Note: It is important to use a good homemade stock as bouillon cubes are not suitable for this recipe.

To garnish with leek rings it is important to blanch the leek first, otherwise the flavor will be too strong: add to boiling water, leave 2 minutes, drain, then refresh under cold running water.

Cheese & Artichoke Chowder

2 tablespoons butter
1 small onion, sliced
1 pound Jerusalem artichokes, sliced
   into water with 1 tablespoon lemon
   juice added
8 ounces carrots, sliced
5 teaspoons all-purpose flour
2-1/2 cups chicken or vegetable stock
1-1/4 cups milk
8 ounces Gruyère cheese, shredded
   (2 cups)
1/2 teaspoon dry mustard
Salt and pepper, to taste

Julienne Garnish:
1 Jerusalem artichoke
1 carrot
1 leek
Chervil leaves

In a large saucepan, melt butter, add onion and cook 1 minute, stirring constantly. Drain artichokes; add to pan with carrots. Cook 2 minutes. Add flour, then gradually add stock. Cover and simmer 20 minutes.

Meanwhile, prepare julienne garnish. Cut artichoke, carrot and green part of the leek into julienne strips. Blanch in boiling water 1 minute; refresh in cold water and set aside.

Blend soup in a blender or food processor fitted with the metal blade until smooth. Add milk, cheese and seasonings and blend again. Pour into a clean pan and reheat gently; do not boil.

Pour into individual soup bowls and garnish with the prepared vegetables and chervil leaves.

Makes 4 servings.

Avocado with Mascarpone

4 avocados, ripe but firm, halved
3 tablespoons freshly squeezed lemon
 juice
4 ounces mascarpone cheese
1 or 2 teaspoons French-style mustard
1 garlic clove, crushed
Few drops hot pepper sauce
Salt and pepper, to taste

To Garnish:
1/4 cup (1 oz.) sliced almonds
Parsley sprigs
Chive flowers (optional)

Carefully scoop out avocado using a teaspoon, making sure skins remain whole; set skins aside. Roughly chop the flesh, put into a bowl and sprinkle with 1 tablespoon of the lemon juice, to prevent discoloration.

In a separate bowl, blend cheese with mustard to taste, garlic and remaining lemon juice. Season with hot pepper sauce, salt and pepper. Add chopped avocado and mix in carefully. Pile into avocado shells and chill about 20 minutes.

Garnish with almonds, parsley and chive flowers if available, and serve in individual dishes.

Makes 8 servings.

Note: This tasty dish can be served, with French bread, as a light lunch for 4 people.

Chaource Mousse & Chive Sauce

4 large crisp lettuce leaves
1 teaspoon butter
1/4 cup chopped button mushrooms
1 celery stalk, very finely chopped
1 shallot, chopped
4 ounces chaource cheese, white rind removed, crumbled
3 tablespoons fromage frais or plain yogurt
2/3 cup cold chicken or vegetable stock
2-1/2 teaspoons gelatin powder, dissolved in 2 tablespoons stock
2 teaspoons snipped chives
2 teaspoons chopped parsley
Pinch of dry mustard
Salt and pepper, to taste

Sauce:
1 egg white
1 tablespoon crème fraîche
1 tablespoon snipped chives

To Garnish:
A few lettuce leaves
Carrot julienne
Melba toast

Put lettuce leaves into boiling water, then immediately into cold water. Drain on paper towels. Use to line 4 oiled ramekins.

In a small saucepan, melt butter, add mushrooms, celery and shallot and cook 1 minute. Remove from heat and set aside.

Put cheese, fromage frais and stock into a blender or food processor fitted with the metal blade and process until smooth. Slowly add dissolved gelatin and blend again. Stir in cooked vegetables, herbs and seasonings.

Spoon the mixture into prepared ramekins, arranging the leaves over the filling to enclose it. Chill until set.

Make sauce a few minutes before serving: in a small bowl, whisk egg white until soft peaks form, fold in crème fraîche and chives.

Turn the mousses onto 4 individual plates and spoon over a little sauce. Garnish with lettuce leaves and carrot. Serve with melba toast.

Makes 4 servings.

Grilled Chèvre with Walnuts

4 (3-oz.) chèvre slices
1/2 head chicory, broken into pieces
Few radicchio leaves, broken into
  pieces
1 head Belgium endive, cut
  diagonally into 1/2-inch slices
Handful of rocket leaves
1/4 cup (1 oz.) chopped walnuts

Dressing:
3 tablespoons walnut oil
2 teaspoons white wine vinegar
1/2 teaspoon honey
Salt and pepper, to taste

Place chèvre on a piece of oiled foil in a broiler pan. Preheat broiler.

Put chicory, radicchio, endive and rocket leaves in a bowl.

Put all dressing ingredients in a small jar with a lid and shake vigorously until blended. Pour over salad, toss thoroughly and arrange on 4 individual plates.

Put the chèvre under preheated broiler 1 to 2 minutes or until melting; place 1 slice on each salad.

Sprinkle with walnuts and serve immediately.

Makes 4 servings.

Note: Chèvre may also be bought in (6-1/2-oz.) rolls. Buy 2 rolls and cut them into 6 slices each. Serve 3 slices per person.

Baked Haloumi in Vine Leaves

8 ounces haloumi cheese
16 to 20 vine leaves, packed in brine
Olive oil

Sauce:
1 tablespoon cornstarch
1-1/4 cups tomato juice
2 teaspoons lemon juice
1/4 teaspoon ground pepper
1/4 teaspoon sugar
1/4 teaspoon ground thyme
1 teaspoon shredded basil leaves

To Garnish:
Basil leaves

Pat haloumi dry with paper towels and cut into 16 to 20 (1/2-inch) slices; divide into small bars and set aside.

Soak vine leaves in a large bowl of cold water 30 minutes to remove brine. Drain, then place one at a time into a large pan of boiling water and blanch 2 minutes. Drain and pat dry with paper towels.

Preheat oven to 450F (230C).

Brush a shallow ovenproof dish liberally with oil.

Place a piece of cheese near stalk end of each vine leaf; fold in sides and roll up to form small packets. Pack stuffed vine leaves closely together in a single layer in prepared dish. Brush generously with olive oil and bake 15 to 20 minutes or until crisp.

To make sauce, blend cornstarch with a little of the tomato juice, stir in remaining juice, then place all sauce ingredients in a heavy saucepan over medium heat. Whisk constantly until thickened.

Serve stuffed vine leaves hot on a pool of sauce, garnished with basil leaves.

Makes 8 to 10 servings.

Note: This dish can also be served with rice as a main course for 4 to 5 people.

Deep-Fried Cambazola

8 ounces firm cambazola (or similar
  blue brie-type cheese)
1/2 cup all-purpose flour
Salt and pepper, to taste
2 eggs
1/2 cup dry bread crumbs
Vegetable oil for deep-frying

To Garnish:
4 plums, sliced

To Serve:
1/2 cup Chinese plum sauce

Using a small sharp knife, remove
white rind and cut cheese into 3/4-
inch cubes.

Season flour with salt and pepper.
Beat eggs in one bowl; put bread
crumbs in another.

Dip cheese cubes in seasoned flour,
coating each piece well; shake off excess. Next dip in beaten eggs, then
bread crumbs to coat well, firmly pat-

ting them into place. Refrigerate 20
minutes.

Fill a deep-fryer one-third full with
vegetable oil and heat to 360F (180C)
or until a 1-inch bread cube turns
golden brown in 1 minute. Using a
slotted spoon, carefully lower cheese
cubes one at a time into hot oil; do not
overfill pan—cook cubes in batches.
Deep-fry 3 to 4 minutes or until gold-
en brown; remove with a slotted
spoon and drain on paper towels.
Serve immediately on warmed plates;
the melted cheese oozes out on stand-
ing. Garnish with sliced plums and a
little Chinese plum sauce.

Makes 4 to 5 servings.

Note: Chinese plum sauce is available
from Chinese stores, some supermarkets and delicatessens.

Roquefort Purses

About 3 sheets filo pastry
1 tablespoon butter, melted
1-1/2 ounces Roquefort cheese, cut
    into 12 cubes
12 chives
Vegetable oil for deep-frying

To Garnish:
Chives

Cut pastry into 24 (3-inch) squares. Pile on top of each other and cover with a slightly damp cloth to prevent drying out.

Brush one square with butter; place another on top to make an 8-pointed star, then brush with butter. Put a cheese cube in the center. Bring up edges of pastry to cover cheese and pinch together into a money bag shape—the butter will help pastry to stick together. Tie a chive around top. Repeat with remaining pastry, cheese and chives.

Heat oil in a deep-fryer to 360F (180C) or until a 1-inch bread cube turns golden brown in 1 minute. Place purses in basket and deep-fry 1 minute or until crisp and golden brown. Drain thoroughly on paper towels.

Garnish with chives and serve immediately on individual plates.

Makes 12 appetizers.

Note: Serve 2 or 3 of these purses as a pretty starter. Or, serve as part of a buffet with drinks.

Blue Brie & Broccoli Flan

Pastry:
2-1/4 cups all-purpose flour
Pinch of salt
5 tablespoons butter, chilled
1 egg yolk
3 to 4 tablespoons cold water

Filling:
6 to 8 ounces broccoli
6 ounces Lymeswold or blue Brie,
   white rind removed
2 tablespoons half and half
3 eggs, beaten
2 tablespoons chopped parsley
Salt and pepper, to taste

To make pastry, sift flour and salt into a bowl; add butter. Using a pastry blender or 2 knives, cut butter into flour until pea-size and well coated with flour. Beat egg yolk with 3 table-spoons water; add to bowl and mix to form a soft dough. Add more water if necessary. Form pastry into a ball and flatten slightly into a round with floured hands. Wrap in plastic wrap and refrigerate 15 minutes.

On a lightly floured surface, roll out pastry and use to line a 9-inch flan pan. Prick base with a fork; refriger-ate 10 minutes.

Preheat oven to 375F (190C).

To make filling, cook broccoli in boiling salted water 5 to 6 minutes. Drain, rinse in cold water, drain thor-oughly, then chop coarsely. Set aside.

Break cheese into pieces and put in the top section of a double boiler set over simmering water. Heat gently until melted. Remove from heat. Beat together half and half and eggs, then blend into melted cheese. Stir in pars-ley and season lightly with salt and pepper.

Arrange broccoli in pastry shell, pour cheese mixture over broccoli and bake in oven 30 to 40 minutes or until lightly browned and a knife in-serted off center comes out clean. Serve warm, with a salad.

Makes 6 to 8 servings.

Asparagus & Salmon Quiches

Pastry:
3/4 cup all-purpose flour
3 tablespoons oatmeal
6 tablespoons butter, chilled
About 2 tablespoons cold water

Filling:
1/2 Camembert cheese
4 ounces smoked salmon
16 asparagus tips, blanched
1 egg
2/3 cup half and half
Salt and pepper, to taste
Red (cayenne) pepper

To Garnish:
Parsley sprigs

Preheat oven to 400F (205C).

To make pastry, place flour, oatmeal and butter in a food processor fitted with the metal blade and process 45 seconds. Add water and process 15 seconds or until pastry holds together. Divide pastry into 4 pieces, roll each out on a floured surface to a 5- or 6-inch circle. Line 4 individual flan pans with dough. Refrigerate while preparing filling.

Cut Camembert into 8 sections; cut each section in half horizontally. Cut salmon into 16 small strips; roll up. Place 4 sections of Camembert in each flan pan, rind side down, and arrange salmon rolls and asparagus tips on top.

Beat egg and half and half together; season with salt, pepper and a little cayenne. Pour into flan pans and bake 25 minutes or until a knife inserted off center comes out clean.

Serve warm, garnished with parsley, with a mixed salad.

Makes 4 servings.

Note: If you do not have a food processor, make pastry by cutting butter into oatmeal and flour.

Smoked Trout Gougère

Filling:
3 smoked trout
2 tablespoons butter
6 ounces celery hearts, thinly sliced
8 ounces asparagus, cut into 1-inch
   pieces
1 tablespoon all-purpose flour
2/3 cup half and half
2 tablespoons chopped parsley
2 tablespoons lemon juice

Choux Pastry:
1/4 cup butter
2/3 cup water
2/3 cup all-purpose flour, sifted
2 eggs plus 1 yolk, beaten
Pepper, to taste
3 ounces Austrian smoked cheese or
   Cheddar cheese, shredded (3/4
   cup)

To Garnish:
1/4 cup (1 oz.) sliced almonds, toasted

Preheat oven to 400F (205C). Butter a large shallow baking dish or 4 individual ovenproof dishes.

First prepare filling. Remove skin and bones from trout; flake flesh into large pieces. Set aside.

In a large saucepan, melt butter. Add vegetables and sauté 1 minute. Stir in flour. Remove from heat and gradually stir in half and half; return to heat and bring to a boil, stirring, until thickened. Add trout, parsley and lemon juice to pan; remove from heat.

To make pastry, in a medium saucepan, melt butter in water over low heat; increase heat and bring to a boil. Remove from heat and add flour all at once; beat with a wooden spoon until dough is smooth and leaves side of pan. Beat in eggs and yolk a little at a time until dough is smooth and shiny. Season with pepper and stir in 2 ounces (1/2 cup) of the cheese.

Spoon choux mixture evenly around edge of prepared dish(es). Fill center with fish mixture; sprinkle with remaining cheese. Bake 30 minutes (20 minutes for individual gougères) until pastry is puffed and golden. Sprinkle with almonds and serve immediately.

Makes 4 servings.

Pizza Quattro Formaggi

Dough:
2 cups all-purpose flour
2 tablespoons butter or margarine
1/2 teaspoon salt
1/4 teaspoon sugar
1 (1/4-oz.) package active dry yeast
  (about 1 tablespoon)
About 1/2 cup warm water
  (120-130F/50C)

Filling:
1 tablespoon butter or margarine
1 small onion, thinly sliced
1 (16-oz.) can tomatoes
1 teaspoon dried leaf oregano
Pepper, to taste

Topping:
2 ounces mozzarella cheese, thinly
  sliced
1 ounce Gorgonzola cheese, crumbled
1-1/2 ounces fontina cheese, sliced
1-1/2 ounces bel paese cheese, sliced
1 (2-oz.) can anchovy fillets, drained,
  or 4 lean bacon slices, cut into
  strips
8 to 12 pitted ripe or stuffed green
  olives

Sift flour into a medium bowl; using a pastry blender or 2 knives cut butter or margarine into flour. Stir in salt, sugar and yeast. Mix in enough warm water to form a soft dough; knead until no longer sticky. Cover bowl loosely with plastic wrap and let rise in a warm place 1-1/2 to 2 hours or until doubled in size.

Meanwhile, prepare filling. In a large skillet, melt butter; add onion. Sauté onion until soft. Stir in tomatoes with their juice, oregano and pepper. Mash thoroughly and cook about 10 minutes, stirring frequently or until thick.

Grease a large baking sheet. Preheat oven to 400F (205C).

In center of baking sheet, press out dough to an 8-inch round. Cover with prepared filling to within 1/2 inch of edge. Cover each quarter of pizza with a different cheese and arrange anchovy fillets and olives on top.

Bake 25 to 35 minutes or until crisp and golden.

Makes 4 to 6 servings.

Spinakopitta

1/2 cup plus 2 tablespoons butter
8 ounces zucchini, thinly sliced
1 pound fresh spinach, shredded
4 green onions, thinly sliced
4 ounces marinated feta cheese (feta with oregano and olive oil), crumbled
2 eggs, beaten
Pepper, to taste
8 sheets filo pastry

Preheat oven to 350F (175C).

In a saucepan, melt 2 tablespoons of the butter; add zucchini. Sauté zucchini 4 minutes. Spoon into a large bowl; add spinach and onions and mix well. Add feta cheese, mix in eggs and season with pepper.

Melt remaining butter; liberally butter a deep 11" x 7" baking pan. Line bottom and sides with 4 sheets of filo pastry, brushing each sheet with melted butter. Spoon vegetable mixture evenly over pastry base; cover with remaining 4 sheets of filo, brushing each with melted butter. Trim; tuck trimmings down inside dish to prevent filling escaping.

With a sharp knife, score top two layers of pastry into squares or diamonds. Cover with waxed paper and bake about 45 minutes or until golden and crisp on top. Serve warm or cold, cut into shapes, with a mixed salad.

Makes 8 servings.

Note: If marinated feta cheese is unavailable, use plain feta and add 2 teaspoons olive oil and 1/2 teaspoon dried leaf oregano when preparing filling.

Cheese & Mushroom Nests

8 ounces purchased puff pastry
Milk to glaze
1 teaspoon sesame seeds

Sauce:
1-1/4 cups milk
1 onion slice
6 peppercorns
1 bay leaf
Pinch of ground mace
1 tablespoon butter
1 tablespoon all-purpose flour
1 teaspoon dry mustard
2 tablespoons half and half
2 ounces Leicester cheese, crumbled

Filling:
2 teaspoons butter
2 shallots, chopped
1 cup sliced mushrooms
2 tomatoes, peeled, seeded and sliced
1 tablespoon lemon juice
1 tablespoon snipped chives
8 quail's eggs, hard-cooked

Preheat oven to 400F (205C).

Roll out pastry and cut into 4 (4-inch) circles. Using a 2-inch-round cutter, mark centers and press halfway through pastry. Rough up edge of each circle with a knife. Brush with milk and sprinkle with sesame seeds.

Put on a dampened baking sheet and bake 15 to 20 minutes or until puffed and golden brown, turning baking sheet around once. Cool on a wire rack. Using a sharp knife, remove center circles; discard.

Meanwhile, make sauce: in a saucepan, combine milk, onion, peppercorns, bay leaf and mace. Bring to scalding point, then set aside 10 minutes to infuse; strain.

In a clean pan, melt butter, stir in flour and gradually stir in strained milk. Bring to a boil and boil 1 to 2 minutes. Remove from heat. Add mustard, half and half and cheese, cover and set aside on a very low heat.

To make filling, in a skillet melt butter; add shallots and mushrooms and cook 2 minutes. Add tomatoes and lemon juice and cook 3 minutes; add chives. Immediately divide among pastry cases. Pour a little sauce over the top and arrange 2 quail's eggs on the sauce; one egg can be halved, if desired. Serve immediately with salad.

Makes 4 servings.

Chicken & Brie Filo Bundles

3 cooked chicken breasts, skinned, boned and thinly sliced
10 ounces blue Brie cheese, rind removed, cut into small chunks
Grated peel of 1 lemon
Juice of 1/2 small lemon
1/2 teaspoon chopped fresh thyme
2 tablespoons chopped parsley
1/4 cup unsalted butter, melted
6 sheets filo pastry, halved

Preheat oven to 400F (205C).

Mix together chicken, Brie, lemon peel and juice, thyme and parsley.

Brush insides of 4 (3-1/2-inch diameter) round molds with melted butter.

Brush one half sheet of filo pastry with butter. Place another half sheet on top at a 45° angle; brush with butter. Top with another half sheet at a 90° angle. Make a fist and mold pastry, butter side in, around it. Push into a prepared mold, allowing surplus around top to stand above mold. Repeat with remaining filo sheets.

Divide chicken mixture into 4 portions and use to fill pastry cases. Bring edges of pastry into center one by one and seal together, but ensure points are sticking upright in a random way. Brush with any remaining butter. Place on a baking sheet and bake 25 minutes or until crisp and browned.

Carefully tip filo bundles out of molds, being very careful not to snap any of the fragile points. Place on baking sheet and return to oven 5 minutes, to brown bottom pastry.

Serve with buttered new potatoes and a mixed green salad.

Makes 4 servings.

Goat's Cheese Soufflé

1/4 cup plus 1 tablespoon butter
1/2 cup all-purpose flour
1-1/4 cups milk
1/4 teaspoon freshly grated nutmeg
Salt and pepper, to taste
4 eggs, separated
5 ounces goat's cheese, crumbled

To Garnish:
Herbs
Salad leaves

Evenly butter an 8-inch soufflé dish and refrigerate to let the butter harden. Preheat oven to 375F (190C).

In a saucepan, melt 1/4 cup of the butter, stir in flour and cook 1 minute, stirring. Remove from heat and gradually blend in milk. Return to heat and cook, stirring or until sauce thickens. Remove from heat and stir in remaining butter, nutmeg, salt and pepper.

Cool a few minutes, then gradually beat in egg yolks. Stir in cheese; heat gently 30 seconds to melt and blend into sauce.

In a bowl, whisk egg whites with a pinch of salt until stiff peaks form. Fold about one-quarter into cheese mixture until thoroughly blended; fold in remaining egg whites.

Pour mixture into chilled dish. Put dish on a baking sheet and bake 30 to 40 minutes or until puffed and golden brown. Serve immediately, garnished with a few herbs and salad leaves.

Makes 4 to 5 servings.

Note: To make individual soufflés, divide the mixture among 4 or 5 individual soufflé dishes and bake 15 to 20 minutes or until puffed and golden brown.

Cheese & Chive Puffs

Choux Pastry:
2/3 cup all-purpose flour
Pinch each of salt and red (cayenne)
** pepper**
1/4 cup (1 oz.) shredded sharp
** Cheddar cheese**
1/4 cup butter
2/3 cup water
2 eggs, beaten

Filling:
2 ounces cream cheese with chives
6 ounces carrots, finely grated

Sauce:
1 bunch watercress
1/3 cup milk
2 tablespoons half and half
1 ounce cream cheese with chives
Salt and pepper, to taste

To Garnish:
Carrot flowers or strips
A few chives
Parsley sprigs

To make pastry, sift flour, salt and cayenne into a bowl. Mix in cheese. Put butter and water in a saucepan and bring to a boil. Remove from heat and immediately beat in flour mixture all at once. Return to low heat and beat vigorously until a soft ball forms and leaves the side of the pan. Cool slightly, then gradually add beaten eggs, beating between each addition. Continue beating until mixture is smooth and glossy; cover and leave until cold.

Preheat oven to 425F (220C). Grease a baking sheet. Pipe or spoon about 16 small mounds onto baking sheet. Bake 15 minutes. Reduce temperature to 375F (190C) and bake 10 to 15 minutes or until puffed and golden. Transfer to a wire rack and slit the side of each puff.

To make filling, blend cheese and carrots in a small bowl; spoon into choux puffs.

To make sauce, put watercress, milk, half and half and cheese in a blender or food processor fitted with the metal blade and process until smooth. Pour into a small saucepan and heat gently. Season to taste.

To serve, put 2 or 3 puffs on each plate with a little sauce. Garnish with carrot, chives and parsley.

Makes 16 puffs.

Gruyère & Chicken Roulade

4 chicken breasts, skinned, boned
4 lean smoked ham slices
4 Gruyère cheese slices
1/4 cup chopped chives
2 tablespoons olive oil
1 garlic clove, crushed
1/4 cup white wine
Salt and pepper, to taste
2/3 cup whipping cream

Preheat oven to 350F (175C).

Slice three-quarters of the way horizontally through chicken breasts, cutting through the rounded edge; open out, cover with plastic wrap and beat with a rolling pin to flatten.

Cover each chicken fillet with a ham slice, then a Gruyère slice. Set aside 1 tablespoon chives; sprinkle rest over cheese. Roll up chicken like a jellyroll; secure with wooden picks or string.

In an ovenproof pan, heat oil; cook chicken rolls gently, turning occasionally or until sealed. Pour off excess oil. Add garlic, wine and seasoning to pan, cover and bake 25 to 30 minutes or until tender. Place roulades on a dish; remove wooden picks or string and keep warm.

Put pan on high heat and boil rapidly to reduce contents slightly; add cream and reserved chives and heat through.

Cut each chicken roulade into 1/2-inch slices and arrange them overlapping on 4 warmed dinner plates. Top with sauce and serve immediately, with a selection of cooked baby vegetables.

Makes 4 servings.

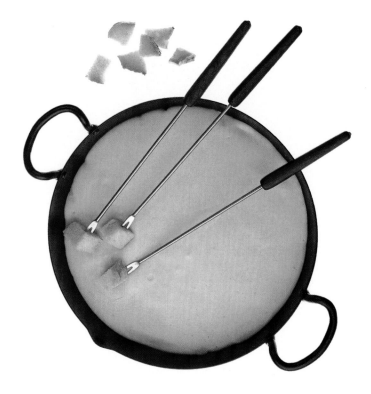

Fondue Suisse

1 garlic clove, halved
1 tablespoon cornstarch
1 cup dry white wine
8 ounces Gruyère cheese, diced
8 ounces Emmenthaler cheese, diced
Pepper, to taste
3 tablespoons kirsch
1 French bread loaf, cut into cubes

Rub cut garlic around the inside of an earthenware fondue dish or heavy pan; discard garlic.

Blend cornstarch with a little of the wine. Pour remaining wine into pan and bring to a boil. Add cheeses and stir until melted and blended.

Add blended cornstarch and pepper and cook about 2 minutes or until mixture combines and becomes creamy; do not boil or the fondue will become stringy. Stir in kirsch.

To serve, keep fondue warm at the table. Divide bread cubes among 4 side plates for the diners, who dip bread into fondue using long-handled forks. Accompany with a chilled dry white wine.

Makes 4 servings.

Garlic & Herb Fondue

1 garlic clove, halved
2/3 cup dry white wine
1 tablespoon cornstarch
1-1/4 cups dairy sour cream
2 (5-oz.) packages full-fat soft cheese
  with garlic and herbs
Pinch of freshly grated nutmeg
Salt and pepper, to taste

To Serve:
1 pound cauliflower, broken into
  flowerets
1 pound broccoli, broken into
  flowerets
Chopped parsley
1 French bread loaf, cut into cubes,
  toasted

Rub cut garlic clove around inside of an earthenware fondue dish or a heavy pan; discard garlic. Add 1/2 cup wine; bring to a boil. Blend cornstarch with remaining wine; add to pan and cook, stirring constantly, until thickened. Reduce heat. Add sour cream and cheese; stir until cheese has melted. Add nutmeg, salt and pepper. Keep warm.

Bring a pan of salted water to a boil, add cauliflower and broccoli and boil 5 to 6 minutes or until crisp-tender. Drain well and place in a warm serving dish.

Sprinkle fondue with parsley and serve immediately with the cauliflower and broccoli and bread cubes.

Makes 4 to 6 servings.

Pine Nut, Pasta & Feta Salad

1-2/3 cups pasta bows
6 bacon slices
1/2 cup (2 oz.) pine nuts
4 tomatoes, peeled, seeded and
  chopped
8 ounces feta cheese, cut into 1/2-inch
  cubes
2 tablespoons torn basil leaves

Dressing:
2 garlic cloves, crushed
2 tablespoons grated Parmesan cheese
2 tablespoons lemon or lime juice
1/4 cup virgin olive oil
1/2 teaspoon Dijon-style mustard
Salt and pepper, to taste

To Garnish:
Basil sprigs

Cook pasta in boiling salted water 10 minutes or until *al dente;* drain under cold water and set aside.

Meanwhile, in a skillet, cook bacon in its own fat until crispy; drain on paper towels, crumble and set aside. Remove all but 1 teaspoon of the bacon fat from skillet. Add pine nuts to pan and cook until golden. Remove from pan and set aside.

To make dressing, combine all ingredients in a jar with a lid and shake until well blended.

Put tomatoes and cheese into a salad bowl; add bacon, pine nuts and basil and mix thoroughly. Add dressing and mix again. Garnish with basil sprigs.

Makes 4 main-dish servings or 6 side-dish servings.

Note: This salad is best tossed in dressing about 20 minutes before serving, to allow flavors to develop.

Haloumi & Sesame Seed Salad

1/2 head radicchio
1/2 head chicory
1/2 bunch watercress
6 ounces haloumi cheese
1 egg, beaten
3/4 cup fresh bread crumbs
Vegetable oil for deep-frying
2 tablespoons sesame seeds, toasted

Dressing:
3 tablespoons virgin olive oil
1 tablespoon wine vinegar
1/2 teaspoon honey
1 teaspoon Dijon-style mustard
1 garlic clove, crushed
Salt and pepper, to taste

To Garnish (Optional):
Nasturtium flowers

Break radicchio, chicory and watercress into bite-size pieces and put into a salad bowl.

To make dressing, mix all ingredients together with a small whisk until blended.

Cut cheese into 1/2-inch cubes and dip into beaten egg; drain thoroughly. Put bread crumbs in a plastic bag, add cheese cubes and toss to coat completely.

Heat oil in a deep-fryer to 360F (180C) or until a 1-inch bread cube turns golden brown in 1 minute and deep-fry cheese in batches until bread crumbs turn golden brown; drain thoroughly on paper towels.

Pour dressing over salad and toss until well coated. Top with fried haloumi and sprinkle with toasted sesame seeds. Serve immediately, garnished with nasturtium flowers, if desired.

Makes 4 servings.

Grape & Gorgonzola Salad

1/2 small melon
8 Romaine lettuce leaves
4 ounces seedless green grapes
3 ounces black grapes, seeded
3 ounces seedless red grapes

Dressing:
6 ounces Gorgonzola cheese,
   crumbled
3 tablespoons mayonnaise
1/4 cup chutney
1/4 teaspoon chili sauce
Squeeze of lemon juice

To Garnish:
Parsley sprigs
Few endive and radicchio leaves
A little paprika

First make dressing: combine all ingredients in a bowl; set aside. Cut melon into 4 slices; remove rind and seeds.

Place 2 lettuce leaves on each of 4 individual plates. Arrange melon and grapes among the leaves.

Put a spoonful of dressing on top of each salad and garnish with parsley, chicory and radicchio leaves. Sprinkle a little paprika over dressing just before serving.

Makes 4 servings.

Note: If a thinner dressing is desired, add half and half or milk until the correct consistency is reached.

Rainbow Salad

1 small red bell pepper
1 small green bell pepper
1 small yellow bell pepper
8 ounces snow peas

Dressing:
3 ounces full-fat soft cheese with
    garlic and herbs
3 tablespoons crème fraîche or dairy
    sour cream
1 tablespoon chopped mixed herbs
Pinch of grated nutmeg
1/4 teaspoon paprika (optional)
Salt and pepper, to taste

To Garnish:
1 tablespoon chopped parsley
1/2 cup (2 oz.) chopped walnuts
A little paprika (optional)

Cut all the peppers into julienne strips. Add the peppers and snow peas to a large pan of boiling water and boil 2 minutes to blanch; drain and refresh in cold water. Arrange the vegetables attractively on a large salad platter, or in individual servings.

To make dressing: in a bowl, mix together cheese and crème fraîche until evenly combined. Stir in herbs, nutmeg, and paprika if using. Add salt and pepper to taste. Spoon dressing on top of salad.

Mix together parsley and walnuts for the garnish and sprinkle on top of the salad. Sprinkle with a little paprika, if desired. Serve immediately as an accompaniment, or with crusty bread as a light meal.

Makes 4 to 6 servings.

Orange & Hazelnut Crepes

Batter:
1/2 cup all-purpose flour
1 small egg
2/3 cup milk
Pinch of freshly grated nutmeg
1 teaspoon vanilla extract
Finely grated peel of 1/2 orange
1 tablespoon vegetable oil

Topping:
8 ounces Grand Marnier cheese
1/4 cup crème fraîche
4 teaspoons finely shredded
    marmalade
2 oranges, peeled, sectioned

Syrup:
2 tablespoons maple syrup
1/4 cup finely shredded marmalade

To Garnish:
Shredded orange and lemon peel
Chopped hazelnuts

To make batter, put all ingredients except oil in a blender or food processor fitted with the metal blade and blend until smooth. Heat a little oil in a small skillet and pour in enough batter to make a crepe 3 inches in diameter. Cook until bubbly on the surface and golden around the edge, then turn and cook the other side until golden. Turn onto waxed paper and keep warm while cooking remaining batter to make 16 crepes in all.

To make topping, mix all ingredients, except the oranges, together in a bowl; set aside.

To make syrup, in a small saucepan, gently heat maple syrup and marmalade until melted and combined. Keep on low heat while assembling crepes.

Put 2 crepes on each of 4 individual plates. Spoon topping over crepes, arrange orange slices around each serving and pour syrup over topping. Decorate with orange and lemon peel and nuts, and serve immediately.

Makes 4 servings.

Note: If Grand Marnier cheese is unavailable, substitute 8 ounces cream cheese and 4 teaspoons Grand Marnier liqueur; omit the crème fraîche.

Store any leftover crepes, tightly wrapped, in the freezer.

Wild Strawberry Creams

1/2 cup whipping cream
3 tablespoons Framboise
1 tablespoon powdered sugar, sifted
3/4 cup fromage frais or plain yogurt
6 ounces wild strawberries

Frosted Leaves:
Strawberry leaves
1 egg white
2 tablespoons superfine sugar

In a bowl, whip cream, Framboise and powdered sugar together until it forms fairly stiff peaks. Fold in fromage frais and all but 12 strawberries. Spoon into 4 dessert dishes and refrigerate 30 minutes.

To make frosted leaves, brush leaves very lightly on both sides with a little egg white; sprinkle with superfine sugar, making sure they are completely coated. Leave in a warm place 30 minutes to dry.

Decorate the creams with remaining strawberries and frosted leaves. Serve with crisp wafer cookies.

Makes 4 servings.

Variations: Use ordinary strawberries instead of wild strawberries and slice them.

Raspberries may also be used in place of strawberries, with frosted raspberry leaves to decorate.

Note: Frosted leaves will last for up to 2 weeks in an airtight container if they are completely coated.

Blueberry Waffles

Topping:
4 ounces Petit Suisse cheese
2 tablespoons whipped cream
1/3 cup powdered sugar, sifted
1 cup blueberries

Batter:
3 cups all-purpose flour
Pinch of salt
1 teaspoon baking soda
1 teaspoon baking powder
2 large eggs
1 cup milk
About 1/2 cup cold water
1/2 cup butter, melted

First prepare topping. Blend together cheese, cream and powdered sugar in a small bowl; set aside.

To make batter, sift dry ingredients into a bowl. Beat eggs and milk together, then gently stir into dry ingredients to form a heavy batter.

Gradually add enough water to make a batter thick enough to coat the back of a spoon; add butter and mix to blend.

Heat an electric waffle iron and brush both sides with oil. Fill one side with batter, clamp down lid and cook until steam ceases to escape and waffles are golden brown and crisp. Remove from iron and keep warm while cooking next waffle.

To serve, put a spoonful of prepared topping on each waffle and cover with blueberries. Serve hot.

Make 2 to 3 servings.

Note: Non-electric waffle irons must be turned over halfway through cooking to ensure even results.

Pashka

1 cup cottage cheese
1/3 cup whipping cream
1 egg yolk
1/4 cup superfine sugar
1/4 cup raisins
1/4 cup finely chopped dried apricots
2 tablespoons chopped mixed nuts
    (walnuts, hazelnuts, almonds)
1 teaspoon vanilla extract
1/2 cup unsalted butter

To Decorate:
Fresh fruit in season

Press cottage cheese through a fine nylon sieve. Put into a large saucepan with remaining ingredients and heat gently 3 to 4 minutes, stirring constantly; do not boil. Remove from heat and let stand until thickened and completely cold.

Pour into prepared container (see below) and put on a rack in a dish, which is big enough to leave a space underneath to catch drips. Cover and refrigerate about 8 hours or until fully drained.

Turn out onto a serving dish and decorate with fresh fruit.

Makes 4 servings.

Note: Pashka is traditionally made in a flowerpot-shaped mold; use a new plastic or clay flowerpot. A sieve or strainer can be used to achieve the required rounded shape. Line chosen mold with cheesecloth or muslin, or use a clean dish towel.

Deep-Baked Cheesecake

1/2 cup butter or margarine
8 ounces graham crackers, finely
    crushed
1/3 cup raspberry jam
3/4 cup fromage frais or plain yogurt
3/4 cup cottage cheese
4 eggs, separated
1/4 cup whipping cream
1/2 cup superfine sugar
1/2 cup all-purpose flour
Juice and grated peel of 1 small
    lemon

To Decorate:
Lemon slices
Lemon peel strips

Preheat oven to 325F (165C).

In a small saucepan, melt butter; stir in crumbs. Press onto bottom of an 8-inch square cake pan. In a small saucepan, warm jam slightly to melt; spread over crumb base. Lightly butter sides of pan.

In a blender or food processor fitted with the metal blade, process cheeses, egg yolks, cream, sugar and flour until blended. Add lemon juice and peel and process briefly.

In a bowl, whisk egg whites until stiff; fold into cheese mixture. Pour onto crumb base and bake 45 minutes to 1 hour or until brown on top and firm to touch. Switch off heat; leave cake in oven 1 to 2 hours or until cool. Remove from oven and leave in pan until completely cold.

To serve, cut into 4 slices, then cut each slice in half. Decorate with lemon slices and lemon peel.

Makes 8 servings.

Chocolate Truffle Cheesecake

12 to 14 ladyfingers
2 tablespoons brandy or rum
1 (8-oz.) package cream cheese,
   softened
1 cup whipping cream
1 teaspoon vanilla extract
12 ounces semisweet chocolate,
   melted
2 egg whites

To Decorate:
2 ounces milk chocolate, melted
2 ounces white chocolate, melted
Rose leaves
1 teaspoon cocoa powder

Line the bottom of a 7-inch spring-form cake pan with waxed paper.

Arrange ladyfingers over paper, cutting them as necessary to fit as tightly as possible. Spoon brandy or rum over ladyfingers.

Beat together cream cheese and cream in a medium bowl until thick; stir in vanilla and chocolate and mix well.

In a bowl, whisk egg whites until stiff; fold into cheese mixture. Spoon into prepared pan; level the top. Cover and refrigerate at least 6 hours to set.

To prepare decoration, brush melted milk and white chocolate onto underside of rose leaves using a fine paintbrush. Place chocolate side up on waxed paper and let set. Apply a second coat and let dry. Carefully lift tip of leaves and peel away from chocolate.

Invert cake onto a serving plate. Using a fine sieve, dust cocoa powder around outside top edge. Arrange chocolate leaves over the top.

Makes 8 to 10 servings.

Note: This dessert is deceptively rich so serve small portions.

Viennese Peach Crescents

1 cup all-purpose flour
1/2 cup unsalted butter, chilled and
  cut into 8 pieces
1/2 cup (4 oz.) curd cheese, beaten
  lightly to soften
8 ounces peach conserve
1 egg yolk beaten with 2 teaspoons
  milk, to glaze

Glacé Icing:
1/2 cup powdered sugar
1 to 2 teaspoons water

Sift flour into a medium bowl. Add butter, scooping flour over each piece to keep separate. Using a pastry blender or two knives, cut in butter until pieces are size of small cherries; it should remain in small lumps, not completely blended into flour. Add cheese and mix to form a dough which just holds together; gather into a ball. Wrap in plastic wrap and refrigerate at least 20 minutes.

On a lightly floured surface, cut pastry in half and roll out each piece to 1/8 inch thickness. Cut into 2-inch squares, then roll out into very thin 3-inch squares. Place a spoonful of conserve on one corner of each square; roll up diagonally from this corner to form a sausage shape. With triangular center flap underneath, curve pastries into crescents. Place well apart on an ungreased baking sheet. Brush with beaten egg yolk. Refrigerate at least 30 minutes or until firm.

Preheat oven to 350F (175C). Bake pastries 15 to 20 minutes or until puffed and golden brown.

To make icing, sift powdered sugar into a bowl. Gradually stir in enough water to make a very thick icing.

Using a paper pastry bag with the end snipped off, pipe a little icing on top of warm pastries. Serve warm.

Makes 16 to 20.

Pineapple Passion Cake

3 pineapple slices, fresh or canned
1 cup butter or margarine, softened
1-1/4 cups superfine sugar
3 eggs, beaten
2 cups self-rising flour
1 teaspoon baking powder
10 ounces carrots, grated
1-1/4 cups (5 oz.) finely chopped
   pecans or walnuts
2 tablespoons lemon juice

Icing:
12 ounces cream cheese, softened
1/2 cup powdered sugar, sifted
1 tablespoon honey

Grease an 8-inch-round cake pan or ring mold. Preheat oven to 350F (175C).

Finely chop one pineapple slice. Divide the other two into tiny wedges and set aside for decoration.

In a bowl, beat butter and sugar together until light and fluffy. Gradu-ally beat in eggs, one at a time. Sift flour and baking powder together; fold into creamed mixture. Stir in chopped pineapple, carrots, three-quarters of the nuts and 1 tablespoon of the lemon juice.

Pour mixture into prepared pan and bake about 1-1/4 hours or until golden and a skewer inserted in the center comes out clean. Reduce tem-perature to 325F (165C) if the cake becomes too brown before it is done. Cool on a wire rack.

To make the icing, cream together cheese, powdered sugar, honey and remaining lemon juice and spread over the top and side of cake. Deco-rate with remaining nuts and re-served pineapple wedges. Let stand a few hours before serving.

Makes 8 to 10 servings.

Cheese & Mustard Bread

1 (1/4-oz.) package active dried yeast
(about 1 tablespoon)
1-1/4 cups warm water (110F/45C)
1-3/4 cups rye flour
2 cups bread flour
1 teaspoon salt
1 tablespoon vegetable oil
6 tablespoons whole-grain mustard
1-1/2 cups (6 oz.) shredded
Emmenthaler cheese
3 tablespoons chopped parsley
1 teaspoon black mustard seeds

Dissolve yeast in 1/4 cup of the water; let stand 5 minutes until frothy. Put flours and salt into a large bowl; make a well in the center. Add yeast mixture, remaining water and oil and mix to a soft dough.

Knead on a lightly floured surface about 5 minutes or until smooth and elastic. Put into a clean bowl, cover with a damp cloth and let rise in a warm place 1-1/2 to 2 hours or until doubled in size.

Preheat oven to 425F (220C).

Punch down dough. Knead dough 2 minutes, then roll into a 12-inch square. Spread with mustard, then sprinkle with cheese and parsley.

Roll up like a jellyroll and place, seam side down, on a floured baking sheet; brush with water and sprinkle with mustard seeds.

Bake 10 minutes; reduce temperature to 400F (205C) and bake 20 minutes or until bread sounds hollow when tapped underneath. Cool on a wire rack.

Makes 1 loaf.

Variation: Use 1 cup light beer instead of 1 cup of the water.

Haloumi & Mint Bread

1 (1/4-oz.) package active dried yeast
  (about 1 tablespoon)
1-1/4 cups warm water (110F/45C)
1-3/4 cups whole-wheat flour
2 cups all-purpose flour
1 teaspoon salt
1 tablespoon olive oil
6 ounces haloumi cheese, diced
3 tablespoons chopped mint
1 tablespoon sesame seeds

Dissolve yeast in 1/4 cup of the water; let stand 5 minutes until frothy. Put flours and salt into a large bowl; make a well in the center. Add yeast mixture, remaining water and oil and mix to a soft dough.

Knead on a lightly floured surface about 5 minutes or until smooth and elastic. Put into a clean bowl, cover with a damp cloth and let rise in a warm place 1-1/2 to 2 hours or until doubled in size.

Preheat oven to 450F (230C). Turn dough onto a floured surface and punch down into a flattish round. Put cheese and mint on top, fold over and knead for about 5 minutes or until cheese and mint are well mixed in.

Shape into a circle and press out into an 8-inch round. Put on a floured baking sheet and make a cut 1 inch from the edge, almost through to the bottom, all the way around. Brush with water and sprinkle with sesame seeds.

Bake 10 minutes; reduce temperature to 400F (205C) and bake 20 minutes or until bread sounds hollow when tapped underneath.

Cool on a wire rack.

Makes 1 loaf.

Index

Amou 72
Annot 72
Appenzeller 60
Asiago 50
Austrian smoked cheese 82; recipe 96

Banon 66
Barac 72
Barbarey 78
Beaufort 60
Beaumont 50
Beenleigh Blue 40
Bel Paese 82
Bergues 30
Bitto 60
Bleu d'Auvergne 40
Bleu de Bresse 40
Bleu des Causses 40
Bleu de Gex 40
Bleu de Sassenage 42
Blue Brie 42; recipes 94, 100
Blue Cheshire 42
Blue Vinny 42
Blue Wensleydale 44
Bonchester 22
Bougon 66
Boursault 26
Boursin 26; recipe 105
Bresse Bleu 40
Brie 22. *See also* Blue Brie
Brillat-Savarin 26
Bûcheron 66

Caerphilly 50
Cambazola 44; recipe 92
Camembert 22; recipe 95
Cantal 50
Carré de l'Est 22
Cashel Blue 44
Castle Ashby 66
Castle Hill 50
Chabichou 66
Chaource 24; recipe 89
Chaumont 30
Cheddar 52
Cheesecakes 114-115
Cheshire 52
Coeur d'Arras 30
Comté 60
Cotherstone 52
Cottage cheese 16; recipes 113, 114
Coulommiers 24
Cream cheese 16; recipes 115, 117
Curd cheese 16; recipe 116

Danish Blue 44; recipe 84
Dauphin 30
Délice de St. Cyr 26
Derby 54
Dit d'Hesdin 38
Dorset Blue 44

Edam 54

Emmentaler 60; recipes 104, 118
Epoisses 30
Estrom 30
Excelsior 28
Exmoor 54
Explorateur 28

Feta 16; recipes 98, 106
Fiore Sardo 72
Fjordland 62
Fontal 54
Fontina 54
Fougeru 24
Fourme d'Ambert 46
Fourme de Montbrison 46
Frinault 78
Fromage Blanc or Fromage Frais 18; recipes 85, 111

Gloucester, double 56; single 54
Gorgonzola 46; recipe 108
Gouda 56
Gruyère 62; recipes 87, 103, 104
Guéret 78

Haloumi 66; recipes 91, 107, 119
Harbourne Blue 46
Heiltz de Maurupt 78
Herrgardsost 62
Huntsman 82
Hurstone 56

Jarlsberg 62

Lanark Blue 46
Lancashire 56
Langres 32
Laruns 72
Leicester 56; recipe 99
Leyden 58
Limburger 32
Livarot 32
Lucullus 28
Lymeswold 48

Magnum 28
Maroilles 32
Mascarpone 18; recipe 88
Mendip Goat 68
Mignot 78
Milleens 32
Mimolette 58
Montrachet 68
Mothais 68
Mozzarella 18
Munster 34
Murol 34
Mycella 48

Nantais 34
Neufchâtel 24
Niolo 74
Noyers le Val 78

Olivet Bleu 79
Olivet Cendré 79
Orangerulle 82

Paneer 18
Pannes Cendré 80
Parmesan 62
Pecorino Romano 74; Siciliano 74
Petit Suisse 20; recipe 112
Pierre Robert 28
Pizza Quattro Formaggi 97
Pont l'Evêque 34
Present 58

Quark 20

Reblochon 34
Remoudou 34
Ribblesdale 68
Ricotta 20
Rigotte de Condrieu 80
Rigotte de Pelussin 80
Roquefort 48; recipe 93
Roulé 82

Saanen 64
Saingorlon 48
Saint-Christophe 68
Saint-Florentin 36
Saint-Marcellin 80
Saint-Nectaire 36
Saint-Paulin 36
Saint-Remy 36
Sainte-Marie 20
Sainte-Maure 70
Samso 64
Sapsago 64
Sarteno 76
Satterleigh 70
Sbrinz 64
Sheviock 74
Sorbais 36
Spenwood 76
Stilton 48

Taleggio 38
Tommes 58, 70, 76, 82
Torville 38
Trappiste de Belval 38
Tymsboro 70

Vacherin 38
Valençay 70
Venaco 76

Wensleydale 58
Wharfedale Blue 48
White Stilton 48; recipe 86
Windsor Red 82